Sophocles' Antigone

Sophocles' Antigone

With Introduction, Translation and Essay
Ruby Blondell
University of Washington

Focus Classical Library
Focus Publishing/R Pullins Company
Newburyport MA 01950

Cover illustration: Athens NM 1170, P. of Bologna 228, ARV^2 512.13, courtesy of the National Museum of Athens.

To my first Greek teacher, Helen Asquith, and my Greek students

κεἴ τις ᾖ σοφός, τὸ μανθάνειν
πόλλ᾽ αἰσχρὸν οὐδέν

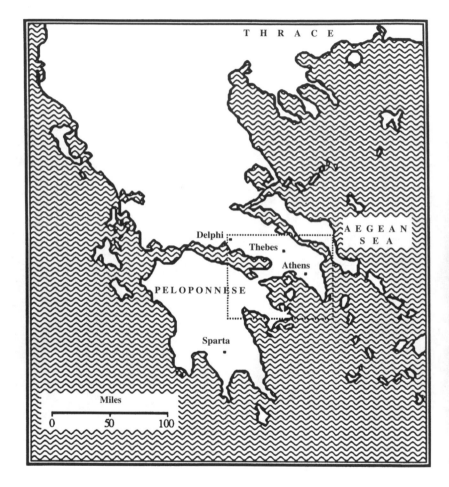

THRACE

AEGEAN
SEA

Delphi
Thebes
Athens

PELOPONNESE

Sparta

Miles
0   50   100

MAINLAND GREECE

Contents

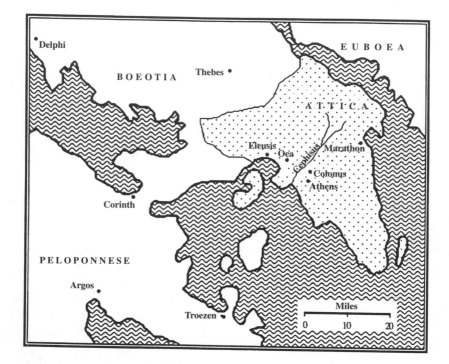

ATTICA AND ENVIRONS

Preface

Sophocles' *Antigone* has been translated countless times. This new translation is aimed at all those, especially students and teachers, who wish to work with an English version that closely follows the Greek original. I have tried to remain reasonably faithful to Greek idiom and metaphor, to translate words important for the meaning of the play consistently, and sometimes to retain the original word order, verse and sentence structure. The original meters have inevitably been sacrificed, but I have used a kind of six-beat iambic line for the iambic (spoken) portion of the drama, and tried to retain an approximately anapestic rhythm for Sophocles' anapests (which are printed in italics). I have not used any formal metrical scheme for the lyrics, which are simply rendered in short lines and indented. (In a few lyric passages the line numbers of the Greek are inconsistent with the number of lines in the text, for reasons of colometry; I have altered the number of lines in the translation in order to avoid confusing the reader.) Despite this attempt to retain some of the rhythmic sense of the original, my first priorities have usually been accuracy and consistency. This approach sometimes leads to awkward moments, but I hope they will be outweighed by its benefits. Though many aspects of the original have been lost, as they must be in any translation, I believe, and hope the reader will agree, that much of the poetry of meaning is best communicated in this way.

The spellings of Greek names attempt to retain some of the benefits of both comfort and defamiliarization. For the most part I have used traditional English spelling for the names of historical persons and places (e.g. Aeschylus, Athens), but transliterated mythological names in so far as this accords with modern English pronunciation (e.g. Kreon, Polyneices). The explanatory notes are aimed at those approaching this play, and perhaps ancient Greek culture, for the first time. They provide factual information on such matters as mythology, geography and unfamiliar cultural practices, together with clarification of obscure phrases and some interpretive pointers. There are no stage directions in ancient Greek texts. Those provided in the translation are based on indications in the dialogue, and are intended to clarify the stage action for the modern reader. A fuller discussion of important background material concerning the poet, his theater and the myth of Oedipus and his family is contained in the Introduction. The translation is followed by an Interpretive Essay, to be read after the play, together with some suggestions for further reading.

The first draft of this translation was based on the Greek of Hugh Lloyd-Jones and Nigel Wilson's Oxford Classical Text (Oxford 1990), but I have departed from their text on occasion. I am especially grateful to Mark Griffith for making available to me his forthcoming edition of *Antigone* for Cambridge University Press. In places I have followed his text, and his notes have been extremely valuable. My translation and notes are also indebted to Jebb's great work,[1] and to a lesser extent to Kamerbeek's more recent commentary.[2] This work was supported in part by sabbatical leave from the University of Washington. I am most grateful to my students, colleagues and friends who read the manuscript and made suggestions for improvement, especially the Focus editors Michael Halleran and James Clauss, my research assistant Pauline Ripat, John Kirby and his mythology students at Purdue, and David Guichard.

University of Washington

1 R.C. Jebb, *Sophocles, the Plays and Fragments. Part III: The Antigone* (3rd edition Cambridge 1900).

2 J.C. Kamerbeek, *The Plays of Sophocles. Commentaries Part III: The Antigone* (Leiden 1878).

Introduction[1]

Sophocles

Of the hundreds of tragedies produced in fifth-century BCE Athens, only a few works by just three dramatists have survived to the present day. Seven of these surviving plays are by the poet Sophocles, who was born at Colonus, the rural village near Athens where his play *Oedipus at Colonus* is set, in about 495 BCE. This makes him a generation younger than his great predecessor Aeschylus (c. 525-456), and ten or fifteen years older than Euripides (c. 480-406). But the relationship between the three tragedians and their works is not strictly linear. The first dozen years of Sophocles' career overlapped with Aeschylus' final years, and for the rest of his long life Euripides was his rival. Aeschylus made use of Sophocles' theatrical innovations (discussed below), and Sophocles in turn was influenced by Euripides. It is said that when Euripides died in 406 BCE, Sophocles dressed his chorus in mourning at a public ceremony which preceded the dramatic festival (the *proagon*). He himself was to die later the same year, or early in 405. In the fourth century and beyond, these three men rapidly became canonized as the great figures of the Athenian tragic theater, which led to the survival of some of their works when the entire output of the other tragic playwrights was lost. As with all ancient texts, the survival of these particular plays depended not only on the vagaries of taste, but on the chancy process of the copying and recopying of manuscripts, until the advent of printing nearly two thousand years later.

Sophocles lived a long and active life, spanning almost the whole of the fifth century BCE, which saw a great many political and cultural achievements at Athens. We know almost nothing of his background (except that his father, Sophillus, is said to have owned a weapons factory), but the evidence of his career suggests a well-connected family. Like any Athenian boy whose father could afford it, he will have received the customary education in music, poetry and athletics. The mainstay of this education was

---

1 Much of this introduction is adapted from my Introduction to *Sophocles' Oedipus at Colonus, Translated with Introduction, Notes and Interpretive Essay* (Focus Classical Library: Newburyport 1990).

Homer, especially the *Iliad*, which was thought to embody not just literary excellence but traditional cultural and moral values. As a boy, Sophocles will have learned to recite large chunks of the epic from memory. This must have been especially significant for the future playwright whom later writers were to describe as "most Homeric" of the tragedians.

The poet's childhood coincided with the Persian Wars, in which the Greeks, largely under the leadership of Athens, repelled two Persian attempts to invade the Greek mainland. Sophocles was about five years old when the Athenians won their first great victory over the Persians at the battle of Marathon (490 BCE). When the Persians were defeated again, in a sea-battle off the island of Salamis in 480 BCE, the young Sophocles is said to have led the victory dance. If true, this was a significant honor, as well as a tribute to the youth's good looks and physical grace. He grew to maturity in the years following the Persian Wars, when the power and influence of Athens were on the rise. After the war the city had founded the Delian League, an alliance of Greek states for mutual defense against the Persians. But as the fifth century progressed Athens took increasing control of the League, until it grew to resemble an Athenian empire rather than an alliance of free states. The subject allies were required to pay Athens large amounts of annual tribute in the form of ships or money. This period of Athenian history is marked by the leadership of Pericles, who was born around the same time as Sophocles and dominated public life from about 460 BCE until his death from the plague in 429. He both strengthened democracy at home and expanded Athenian influence abroad, in large part by exploiting Athenian leadership of the Delian League.

One of Pericles' most ambitious enterprises was a public building program which culminated in the construction of the Parthenon—the great temple of Athena on the Acropolis at Athens. Like other such projects, this temple, with its magnificent architecture and sculptural decoration, was partly financed by taxes from members of the Delian League. Besides his support for the visual arts, Pericles was a patron of writers and thinkers, helping to promote the extraordinary artistic and intellectual accomplishments of fifth-century Athens. Literary excellence was also fostered by the generally open and tolerant nature of the Athenian democratic ideal, which placed a high value on artistic achievement and freedom of expression. (It is worth remembering that Socrates was active as a provocative "gadfly" throughout most of this period, and was not prosecuted until 399 BCE, after Athens had become demoralized by defeat and less tolerant of public criticism.) But the cultural achievements of Periclean Athens meant little to the oppressed members of its empire or to its rivals, headed by Sparta. In 431 BCE, when Sophocles was in his sixties, the resentment aroused by Athenian expansion culminated in the outbreak of the Peloponnesian War, between Athens with its allies on one side and Sparta with its allies on the other. This long and draining war dominated the last twenty-five years of the poet's life, and he was to die before it finally ended in the defeat of Athens in 404 BCE.

Sophocles began his dramatic career in 468 BC with a group of four plays which have not survived (one of them was called *Triptolemos*). He defeated Aeschylus to win first prize in the tragic competition (on which see further below). By this time tragedy in Athens had already developed into a mature art form. But the conventions of the genre were not static, and Sophocles had a reputation in antiquity as a theatrical innovator. Aristotle tells us in the *Poetics* that he increased the number of actors from two to three, and introduced the practice of scene painting. He is also said to have enlarged the size of the chorus from twelve to fifteen, written a book on dramaturgy, and founded an artistic society dedicated to the Muses (the patron goddesses of music and the arts). In the course of his long career he wrote more than 120 dramas—about 90 tragedies and 30 satyr plays (a kind of mythological burlesque). Of this enormous output we have only seven tragedies, significant parts of two satyr plays and some scattered fragments. The survival of these particular plays was not random, but probably resulted from their conscious selection as Sophocles "best" plays, in somebody's opinion, at some point in the process of transmission.

Of the surviving tragedies we have secure production dates for only two, which also happen to be the last of the seven: *Philoctetes*, produced in 409 BCE, and *Oedipus at Colonus*, produced posthumously in 401. *Oedipus the King* was probably produced somewhere between 430 and 425. The dating of *Ajax*, *Electra* and *Women of Trachis* is highly speculative. *Antigone* may have been produced about 442 BCE. The evidence for this is insecure, however. An ancient commentator tells us that Sophocles was elected general for the Samian war (which began in 441) because of the admiration aroused by this play. We know from other evidence that Sophocles did indeed hold such a post, serving with Pericles during the Samian revolt of 441/440. The idea that he was elected on the strength of *Antigone* is thought by most scholars to be dubious, like many stories concerning the lives of ancient poets; but it is not impossible, given the ancient Athenians' belief in the educational value of poetry, and the explicitly political subject matter of *Antigone*. (A fourth-century orator was to quote Kreon's speech with approval for its patriotic content; cf. Essay p. 81.) Even if the story is untrue, however, it was probably fabricated precisely because the play preceded the generalship rather closely. But *Antigone* could not have been produced in 441, since the election preceded the dramatic festival. So a hypothetical date, usually accepted for lack of any other evidence, is 442.

Whether or not we believe that *Antigone* secured Sophocles' election as general, this story indicates both the high regard in which a popular poet might be held, and the lack of a sharp dichotomy between achievement in artistic and political life. As his service as general illustrates, Sophocles took an active part in the political, military and religious life of

Athens, in line with cultural expectations for male citizens of the leisured classes. An anecdote about this military campaign helps bring him to life for us. When Pericles remarked one night at a party that Sophocles was a good poet but a bad strategist, he displayed his strategic expertise by stealing a kiss from a handsome boy who was pouring the wine. Another story, from Plato, recounts that Sophocles was relieved to be freed by old age from the tyranny of sexual desire for women (*Republic* 329bc). Such anecdotes suggest an urbane and passionate man who participated in the wide range of activities—political, social, erotic—expected of his gender, class and culture.

Besides serving as general, Sophocles held the important office of public treasurer in 443/2. Late in life he was again chosen for significant public office. In 413 BCE Athens suffered a crushing defeat in Sicily, and the poet (now more than eighty years old) was one of ten commissioners appointed to reorganize Athenian affairs after the crisis. Another incident shows him participating in a different area of public life. In 420 BCE the cult of Asklepios, god of medicine, was formally introduced into Athens. The god, who took the form of a snake, remained in the house of Sophocles until his official residence could be prepared. For this service the poet was honored with a cult after his death.

Sophocles was probably acquainted with many of the most important cultural figures of his day. Besides the association with Pericles, his name is connected with such people as the philosopher Archelaus (the teacher of Socrates), and the historian Herodotus. Both *Antigone* and *Oedipus at Colonus* provide evidence for his familiarity with Herodotus' work. When Oedipus compares his sons to the Egyptians, whose customs are said to be the opposite of the Greeks' (*OC* 337-41), he is probably drawing on the colorful account in the second book of Herodotus' *Histories* (2.35). And when Antigone explains that she buried her brother because, unlike a child or husband, he is irreplaceable, she is echoing an argument from Herodotus (see note on line 908, and Essay, p. 95-6).

The plays of Sophocles also show an unmistakable familiarity with rhetorical techniques popularized by the contemporary thinkers known as "sophists." These itinerant intellectuals offered instruction in many subjects, and were associated with relativism and other intellectual challenges to traditional moral and religious values. Their principle subject, however, was rhetoric, for which they found a ready audience at Athens, where public life was pervaded by debate and persuasive speaking was the key to political success. In the Athenian democracy public policy was decided by an assembly open to all adult male citizens, who voted on each issue after extensive debate. Athenian society was also highly litigious, and a citizen had to plead his own case in court before a jury of several hundred of his peers. It is therefore not surprising that the dramatists and their audience had a highly developed appreciation for this kind of oratory. Though

Sophocles' style may seem less self-consciously rhetorical than that of Euripides, the influence of public oratory can clearly be seen, especially in the long and formal speeches with which his characters often debate each other.

Sophocles lived to the age of about ninety. The story goes that in his advanced old age he quarreled with his son Iophon, who then sued him for senility under a law allowing a son to take control of an incompetent father's property. In his own defense, Sophocles read aloud in court from the play he was working on at the time: the opening lines of the song in praise of Attica from *Oedipus at Colonus* (668-93). Naturally he was acquitted. Like most such stories, this one is unlikely to be true. (It is probably derived from a contemporary comedy lampooning the poet and his son.) But it tells us something about the image of Sophocles that was constructed even at an early date. He did not attract such colorful anecdotes as many other public figures, including the other two major tragedians. (Aeschylus was supposedly killed by a tortoise dropped on his head by an eagle, and Euripides was said to be a misanthropic cave-dwelling vegetarian torn apart by hunting dogs.) This accords with the way he is presented by the comic playwright Aristophanes. In Aristophanes' play *Clouds*, Aeschylus and Euripides are used to embody stuffy traditionalism and new-fangled immorality respectively, with no mention at all of Sophocles (*Clouds* 1364-72). Likewise in Aristophanes' *Frogs*, Aeschylus and Euripides are polarized and pilloried as exemplars of extreme styles of drama—the old-fashioned and the new-fangled respectively—while Sophocles is said to have been a good-tempered man in life and death (*Frogs* 82). We may also note that his style is much harder to parody than that of either of the other two. All this suggests that Sophocles was elided from the competition of the *Frogs* in part because of his apparently "moderate" qualities, both personal and poetical. The fact that his year of birth falls between the other two poets has further encouraged this Aristophanic picture of him as a kind of "mean" between the other two tragedians.

From earliest times, then, Sophocles has been constructed as the most "serene" and "ideal" of the dramatists, the one who aimed at and achieved alleged classical canons of moderation and harmony. This reputation was cemented in later years by Aristotle's canonization of *Oedipus the King* as the ideal tragedy in his enormously influential *Poetics*. The idealization of Sophocles as the quintessential classical Greek tragedian has continued to the present day, encouraged, among other things, by Hegel's influential use of *Antigone* and Freud's of *Oedipus the King*. In some ways, this idolatry has benefited the study of Sophocles. But in other ways it has damaged it, by casting an aura of sanctity or dusty respectability over his works, enshrining them as "classical" and therefore unexciting or impervious to criticism. It is best to approach his plays with an open mind, paying close attention to the texts themselves and their cultural context, and remaining alert to the biases introduced, whether consciously or otherwise, by our own cultural accretions.

Theater and performance[4]

The form of drama that we call "Greek" tragedy was in fact a peculiarly Athenian art form, closely associated with the life of Athens in the fifth century BCE. We know of nothing quite like it in other Greek states of the period. It was enormously popular, in a way which may be hard to grasp today, drawing audiences of 15,000-20,000 out of a citizen body of only about 300,000 men, women and children (including slaves and resident aliens). There is no modern equivalent of the Athenian dramatic performances. They combined the official status of a public institution (both civic and religious), the broad popularity of a Hollywood blockbuster, the emotional and competitive appeal of a major sporting event, and the artistic and cultural pre-eminence of Shakespeare. The theater was so far from being an elitist form of entertainment that a fund was instituted to enable poor citizens to buy tickets.

The exact composition of the audience is, however, a matter of controversy. In particular, scholars are not entirely agreed on whether women were permitted to attend. The traditional assumption that they could not is based on the general exclusion of women from most public arenas of Athenian life. But the main exceptions to this exclusion were religious. Women were able, and indeed required, to go out in public for such events as religious festivals and funerals. And the dramatic festivals were ritual occasions (see further below). Moreover Dionysos, in whose honor these plays were performed, was a god whose myths and cult embraced all kinds of outsiders. In contrast to most major male divinities, women played an important part in his cult. This accords with what little concrete evidence we have, which suggests that women, along with other socially marginal groups, including even slaves, were indeed permitted to attend the theater. It seems likely, however, that these socially inferior groups would have been present in much smaller numbers than the male citizens who were the dramatists' primary audience.

Drama at Athens was produced only at public festivals in honor of Dionysos. This god is associated with song and dance, masking and shifting identities, wine and irrational frenzy, vegetation, sex, fertility, sensuality and growth. He is thus an apt patron for an art form that celebrates the crossing of boundaries and the playing of roles. It was at his principal Athenian festival, the City Dionysia, that most of the great tragedians' works

---

4   An expanded version of this section will appear in the general introduction to *Women on the Edge: Four Plays by Euripides*, translated with introductions and commentary by Mary Whitlock Blundell, Mary-Kay Gamel, Nancy Sorkin Rabinowitz and Bella Zweig (Routledge: New York, forthcoming). For a full discussion, with ancient sources translated into English, see Csapo and Slater 1995.

were first performed. At the beginning of the festival a statue of the god was carried in a torchlight procession to the theater, and it remained present throughout the dramas. But the plays were not religious rituals in any modern sense. Drama may have arisen from ritual, and often makes use of ritual forms such as sacrifice, wedding and funeral rites (all of which are important for *Antigone*). But drama was not *itself* a ritual. Playwrights and performers were, of course, honoring the gods by their work, but there is no suggestion in our sources that the results were evaluated by religious criteria.

The festival of Dionysos, which lasted several days, included processions, sacrifices, and musical and dramatic performances of various kinds. It was a major civic as well as religious celebration, an occasion for public festivity and civic pride, and an opportunity for Athens to display itself and its cultural achievements—including drama itself—to the world. The City Dionysia took place in the spring, when the sailing season had begun and visitors from all over the Greek world might be in town, including the members of the Delian league, who brought their tribute to Athens at this time of year. This tribute was displayed in the theater during the festival. Other related ceremonies included the awarding of golden crowns to public benefactors and the presentation of sets of armor to young men whose fathers had been killed in battle. All this provides striking evidence for the political context of Athenian drama. We should bear this in mind when seeking to understand a play such as *Antigone*, whose primary themes include the relationship of the individual to society at large and the proper conduct of a ruler. The primary subject matter of tragedy is traditional mythology, but this material is used to scrutinize the political and cultural ideology of the poets' own time, including democracy, gender norms, and Athenian identity.

The tragedies at the City Dionysia were produced as part of a competition. Greek culture generally was highly competitive, and religious festivals often involved various kinds of contest. The Olympic games are one prominent example, and the City Dionysia itself included contests in comedy, a satyr play and choral song as well as tragedy. The tragic competition lasted for three days, with each poet producing three tragedies followed by one satyr play in the course of a single day. Sometimes the tragedies would constitute a connected trilogy, like Aeschylus' *Oresteia*, and even the satyr play might be on a related theme. But Sophocles seems to have preferred individual, self-contained dramas. The five judges who decided the contest were carefully selected by an elaborate procedure designed to prevent undue influence and bribes, and their decision was made under pressure from a highly rambunctious crowd. The winning playwright and *chorēgos* (see below) were publicly announced, crowned with ivy (a plant sacred to Dionysos), and had their names inscribed on a marble monument. Sophocles was extremely successful, winning at least eighteen victories and never coming third in the competition.

Since only three playwrights were allowed to put on their plays at each festival, even having one's plays produced was a competitive challenge. In keeping with the public nature of the event, a city official was in charge of "granting a chorus" to three finalists out of those who applied (how he reached his decision is unknown). A wealthy citizen (the *chorēgos*) was appointed to bear most of the production costs, as a kind of prestigious extra taxation. Chief among these costs was the considerable expense of training and costuming the chorus. The poet was his own producer, and originally acted as well, or employed professional actors, (Sophocles is said to have been the first to stop acting in his own plays, allegedly because of the weakness of his voice.) But around the middle of the fifth century the state also assumed control of allocating a principal actor to each produc-

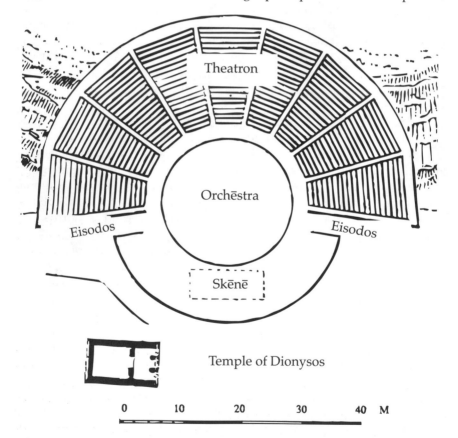

A reconstruction of the theater of Dionysus in Athens during the second half of the fifth century BC. (Based on the sketch by J. Travlos, *Pictorial Dictionary of Ancient Athens* [London 1971] 540.)

tion, and began awarding a prize for the best actor.

The plays were performed in the open-air theater of Dionysos on the south-eastern slope of the Acropolis, where an impressive view of the temple of Dionysos, backed by the mountains and coastline of southern Attica, stretched beyond the playing area. Performances began at dawn and lasted all day. Some plays, including *Antigone*, begin at dawn, which may be an allusion to daybreak in the actual theater. Once the sun had risen, the size and openness of the theater were enhanced by the bright daylight enveloping performers and audience alike. This generated a very different and specifically more public atmosphere than the darkened theaters and artificial lighting of today. The audience must have been very conscious of each other as well as the play, and thus aware of their collective engagement in a public civic event. They sat crowded together, expressed their opinions vociferously, and ate and drank during the performances, especially if they did not approve of the acting. They responded to the plays with visceral emotion, judging them not as aesthetic artefacts remote from real life, but as contributions to the discussion of contemporary political, moral and social concerns. The theater was an extension of their world, not an escape from it.

The theater of Dionysos resembled one end of a large football stadium in size and shape (see diagram, p. 8). The judges sat in carved stone seats at the front, along with the priests of Dionysos and other religious figures, public benefactors, high-ranking officials and important foreign vistors. Most of the audience probably sat on the ground, on the sloping sides of the Acropolis hill above the theater. Foreigners, women, children and slaves were probably seated at the back and sides of the theater. The performance area was dominated by a large dancing floor, the *orchēstra*, which was about seventy feet across. Contemporary scholars are divided over the shape of the *orchēstra* in Sophocles' time. (It may have been round or rectangular.) Behind it was a wooden stage-building, the *skēnē* (literally "tent" or "hut") which served as a set. Whether or not there was a raised stage in the fifth century is also a matter of controversy. If so, it was merely a low, narrow platform in front of the stage-building.[5] The *skēnē* had one or more doors through which characters could enter and exit, and was also used by the actors as a changing-room. It usually represents a palace or other structure (as in *Antigone*), but may also serve, for example, as a cave (as in Sophocles' *Philoctetes*), or a grove (*Oedipus at Colonus*). We do not know to what extent such locations were indicated through scene painting or props, but any such indicators were probably stylized and minimal. The theater was so large that detailed scenery would not have been easily visible.

The main action always takes place outside the stage-building, though interior scenes and scenes from distant locations are often described by the

5 For convenience, however, it is usual in discussing Greek drama to use the word "stage" to refer to the entire performance area, and I have followed that practice.

players. Occasionally an interior scene is revealed through the *skēnē* door, usually at a climactic moment (as at *Antigone* 1293). Sometimes this was accomplished in performance by means of a device called the *ekkuklēma*, a low wheeled platform which might be rolled out of the *skēnē* to display a tableau from within. This device may have been used at the end of *Antigone*. Entrances and exits not involving the *skēnē*, including the entry and departure of the chorus, were made along the *eisodoi* or side-entrances—two long ramps, one on each side of the *orchēstra*. The same *eisodos* is used consistently throughout the play to represent a particular locale. In *Antigone*, one of them leads outside the city, to the upland plain where the battle took place and Polyneices lies unburied, and the other to the city of Thebes proper. The house embodies the hidden world of the female (see Essay, p. 76, 89, 103). It stands at a crossroads between battlefield and city, the two main arenas of public male activity. The dominant presence of the palace and the length of the side-entrances could both be exploited for dramatic purposes, as when Kreon consigns the two girls to the house (578-9), the Guard makes his hesitant first entrance (223-32), and Antigone is finally led away.

The entire "production team" of Athenian tragedy (playwrights, producers, dancers, musicians, chorus and actors) were male. This extends to the numerous female roles, all of which were played by adult men. The sex, age and status of each character were indicated in a formal, stylized way by costumes and masks. The masks were bold in design, as they had to be if they were to be visible to spectators seated at the far edge of the theater. But they were naturalistic in manner, covered the whole head, including the ears, and had wigs attached. The lavish costumes included long, colorfully decorated robes, and sometimes tall, thin-soled boots. (Grotesque masks and thick-soled "buskins" came later.) Details of costume and props would make clear the status of each character and might reflect familiar Athenian activities. A king like Kreon would carry a scepter, the blind old Teiresias would wear priestly garb and lean on a staff, and Antigone and Ismene may be dressed in mourning.

The standard number of speaking actors in a given production, apart from the chorus, was three, though there were usually several non-speaking extras playing silent parts such as guards and attendants. The reasons for this restriction to three speaking actors is unknown. But it explains why there are never more than three speaking characters on stage together. It also means that when, as in most plays, there are more than three speaking characters, at least one actor would have to play more than one part. Sometimes, too, a single role had to be split between two or more actors. The latter practice is alien to the conventions of modern drama, but it was facilitated by the fact that the actors were all male, and wore not only distinctive costumes but rigid masks which identified each character clearly. Moreover the acting was highly stylized, and did not rely on subtle body movements or facial expressions (which were ruled out by the masks). In such a large theater the actors must have delivered their lines loudly and emphatically, and used broad, clear gestures, in order to be seen and heard.

A central feature of all Athenian tragedies is the chorus, a group of fifteen performers who normally remain present from their entrance until the end of the play. Its members were masked and dressed in character like the main actors. The choral identity is a collective one. In contrast to the heroic individuality of the actors, the chorus are numerous and anonymous. They have no individual names, and they speak and are addressed indiscriminately in the singular or plural. They therefore represent to a certain extent the group, showing the effects of the main actors' words and deeds on the larger human community. As a collective group, they are in a sense continuous with the audience whose fellow-citizens they are. But whether we view them as actors or citizens, they form only one segment of the community as a whole. As citizens, they are free adult male Athenians playing a role in the theater. But in their dramatic persona they represent, remarkably often, a socially marginal segment of society—women, old men, foreigners, underlings or even slaves. They are thus far from being an embodiment of the *polis* or "society" in the abstract. Even in *Antigone*, where they do play the role of elite males, the chorus are white-haired old men (216, 281, 1092-3), who are explicitly distinguished from the city as a whole (164-9).

Nor does the chorus represent an "objective" view of events or the "voice of the poet." As a character in the drama they have a clearly defined identity, a specific gender and social status, which give them a specific point of view and are important for a proper understanding of the play. Though played by men, their characters are generally of the same sex as the central figure of the drama, with whom they enjoy a certain solidarity. *Antigone* is unusual in this regard, if we regard Antigone herself as the central character (see Essay p. 80, 100). The chorus is sometimes important to the story (as in Aeschylus' *Eumenides*), but is more usually peripheral to the central plot. We do not know how much physical contact took place between chorus and actors, or to what extent they shared the same performance spaces. Sometimes the chorus seem to participate quite vigorously in the stage action (e.g. *Oedipus at Colonus* 829-43). But their dramatic effectiveness is usually quite limited. Their "personality" is also more fluid than that of the main characters, as they react to unfolding events. The chorus of *Antigone* are exceptionally ineffectual and wishy-washy in their attitudes (see further Essay p. 82-3). At the same time, they often serve as a lens through which the audience may focus their own shifting emotional responses.

The primary dramatic medium of the chorus is lyric song and dance, performed in the *orchēstra* or "dancing area." At intervals throughout the drama they perform a choral song, singing and dancing in unison. Although we know little about the choreography, it certainly included a strong mimetic element and drew on the rich living tradition of public choral dance, which was an integral part of many ritual, competitive and festal occasions in ancient Greek life. The accompanying music was simple and did not interfere with comprehension of the words, which are always significant for the drama and sometimes of the highest poetic complexity. Such profundity may at times seem inappropriate to the chorus when viewed in character, e.g. as a group of sailors or slave women. But choral lyrics give the poet a different dramatic idiom in which to explore the themes of the play, and should not be tied too closely to the specific character of the chorus that gives them utterance.

Greek tragedy is structured around the alternation of speech and song. Most plays open with a spoken monologue or dialogue by the actors (called the prologue), which sets the scene and provides the audience with any necessary background information. Sophocles characteristically accomplishes this exposition through conversation, which also serves to introduce important characters. This opening scene is followed by the arrival of the chorus, who enter singing the *parodos* or "entry song." They normally remain in the *orchēstra* for the rest of the play, performing further songs with dancing (known as *stasima* or "songs in position") between the scenes of the drama, and participating to some extent in the action. This alternation of actors' speech and choral song is a fluid form rather than a rigid structure. Actors will sometimes shift into lyric meters, or converse with the chorus in a sung dialogue, especially at moments of high emotion (such as Antigone's last exit or Kreon's final scene). Such a dialogue may play the scene-dividing role of a choral ode, or serve to vary the tone of a long scene. Conversely the chorus had a leader (the *koruphaios*), who not only led the dancing but exchanged a few spoken lines with the actors, serving as the mouthpiece of the chorus as a whole.

Both the spoken and the sung portions of Athenian drama are composed in verse. Greek poetry is not structured through rhyme, but depends on rhythmic patterns (meters) to create poetic form. The lyric songs are composed in highly varied and elaborate meters, unique to each song. A typical choral ode consists of a series of pairs of stanzas called the "strophe" and "antistrophe." Each strophe has its own complex rhythmic structure, which is repeated precisely in the antistrophe. There may be several such strophic pairs, each metrically unique. Occasionally the strophe and antistrophe will echo each other linguistically or structurally as well as metrically (compare *Antigone* 359 with 370, and 614 with 625). The strophic pair may be followed by an epode—an additional stanza with its own unique metrical pattern (as at *Antigone* 876-82). Though the spoken portions of Greek drama may be highly emotional, for example in the rhetorical expression of anger, lyrics are most often the vehicle for intense emotions such as grief, joy or pity, which they express in a more impressionistic, less rational style than spoken dialogue.

The actors' spoken lines, by contrast, are in iambic trimeters, a regular six-beat meter approximating the flow of natural speech (rather like Shakespearean blank verse). Other meters are occasionally used, especially anapests, a regular "marching" rhythm often associated with entrances and exits. Anapests were probably chanted rather than spoken or sung. In *Antigone* they are used unusually often for the announcement of a character's entrance. (They are printed in italics in the translation.) The actors' spoken speeches range in length from the long rhetorical oration, or *rhēsis*, to *stichomythia*, a formal kind of dialogue in which the characters exchange single alternating lines, or occasionally two lines apiece. Such modes of speech, like many other aspects of Greek tragedy, may strike the modern audience as artificial. But every kind of drama relies on its own formal conventions. We tend not to notice the artificiality of our own theater (including film and television) because familiarity makes its conventions seem natural to us.

Mythic Background

The principal subject matter of Athenian tragedy is traditional Greek mythology. But there was no official canon of such tales, and no requirement that various versions should be consistent. The dramatists and their audiences were exposed to many versions of the myths, oral and written, traditional and innovative, in varying contexts which affected their mode of presentation and their meanings (epic recitation, theatrical performance, religious ritual, oral tale-telling, and so on). The tragedians and other writers were also free to create their own innovations in the stories. Some central features of the myths may have been in practice unchangeable (the Greeks always win the Trojan war), but the degree of possible variation that remains may surprise the modern reader (e.g. Helen does not necessarily go to Troy). And even when the stories used are familiar ones, a dramatist was free to vary the characters, for example by making a traditional personality more or less sympathetic. Mythology was therefore a highly flexible medium for the ancient dramatists, enabling them to draw on past traditions and present expectations while adding their own developments to the future store of tales. But our own knowledge of these rich and varied traditions is scanty. It remains helpful for our understanding of the plays to reconstruct as best we can any versions that we know to have been current in the poet's own day. Yet we must bear in mind that countless stories unknown to us undoubtedly influenced the dramatists' practice and helped to shape their meanings for their original audience.

Very little is known of Antigone's story prior to Sophocles. But she is a daughter of Oedipus, the most famous mythic king of Thebes, whose family

---

6 For a detailed account of the mythic background and probable Sophoclean innovations in this play see the introduction to Mark Griffith's edition of *Antigone* (Cambridge University Press, forthcoming).

history formed the subject of several lost epic poems and was an extremely popular subject in poetry and art, both before and during Sophocles' lifetime.[6] Sophocles himself composed three surviving dramas about this family and the terrible events that befell it: *Antigone, Oedipus the King,* and *Oedipus at Colonus.* These plays exemplify the tendency of Athenian tragedy to locate disturbing mythological events outside of Athens itself. Very often such events are located at Thebes, a historical enemy of Athens, which serves as a kind of ideological alter ego or "anti-Athens." As such it is used to embody and explore cultural tensions that might be highly disturbing if dramatized in an Athenian setting. Athens itself, by contrast, is usually irreproachable in Athenian drama.[7] In *Oedipus at Colonus,* for example, Athens under its idealized king Theseus serves as an enlightened and generous haven of refuge for Oedipus, after he has been exiled by the Thebans.

Like Aeschylus' *Oresteia,* Sophocles' three "Theban plays" focus on the doings and sufferings of a single royal family over more than one generation. Unlike the *Oresteia,* however, they are not a trilogy. The three plays of the *Oresteia* (the only trilogy that survives) were composed to be produced together in a single performance, following in sequence the fortunes of the house of Atreus. But Sophocles' three plays were written at wide intervals, without following the legendary order of events. Each is a dramatic unity, and they were never intended to be performed together. Further, in some respects the plays are inconsistent with each other. Yet allusions in the two later plays show that Sophocles had not forgotten, and perhaps hoped that his audience would remember, the thematic threads that connect his three Theban dramas. *Antigone* is very probably the earliest of these plays to have been produced (above, p. 3). But it is the latest in the mythological sequence of events. Accordingly, we may recapture some of the mythic background to the play from Sophocles' other two "Theban" plays, even though they were written later. This is helpful in filling out the story, since we have almost no earlier evidence about her. But it should be done only with great caution. The later plays are not concrete evidence for the background of the earlier. There is, for example, no sign in *Antigone* of Oedipus' exile from Thebes or subsequent transformation into a cult hero. Ismene says their father died "hated and in ill-repute" (50), Antigone declares that she laid him out for burial, presumably at Thebes (897-902), and there is no suggestion of the miraculous death dramatized in *Oedipus at Colonus.*

Oedipus himself is most familiar to the modern mind as the hero of Sophocles' *Oedipus the King,* who falls from the pinnacle of human accomplishment to the depths of an excruciating self-awareness, blinding him-

---

7 On this issue see Zeitlin 1990, with M. W. Blundell, "The Ideal of the *Polis* in *Oedipus at Colonus,*" in *Tragedy, Comedy and the Polis,* ed. A.H. Sommerstein, S. Halliwell, J. Henderson and B. Zimmermann (Bari, Italy 1993) p. 287-306. The only surviving drama in which an Athenian king behaves dubiously is Euripides' *Hippolytos,* which is not set in Athens itself.

self when he discovers that he has unwittingly killed his father, Laios, and married his own mother, Jokasta. He has become a universal symbol not only of the tragic blindness of the human condition, but also, thanks to the incalculable influence of Freud, of the deepest and most terrible fears and desires of the unconscious. The earliest myth of Oedipus, however, makes him no such figure of doom. There was an epic on the subject (now lost). The very little we know suggests that it diverged considerably from the tragedians. In the *Odyssey* we hear that though Oedipus was distressed at the discovery of his deeds, he went on ruling at Thebes (11.271-80). There is no mention of his self-blinding, though his mother/wife hanged herself. The *Iliad* mentions that he died violently—perhaps in battle or a fight— and was honored at Thebes with funeral games (23.679-80).

Oedipus the King opens upon Oedipus as King of Thebes, beloved by his people, an intelligent, confident and compassionate man in the prime of life. We learn in the course of the play that he was raised in Corinth, but left that city in an attempt to evade a prophecy from Apollo's oracle at Delphi that he was to murder his father and marry his mother.[8] Before reaching Thebes he was provoked by an unknown man at a fork in the road, and killed him. Travelling on to Thebes he found the city terrorized by the Sphinx, a winged monster with a woman's head and a lion's body, who killed all those who could not answer her riddle. Oedipus solved the riddle and saved the city. In gratitude, the Thebans gave him the crown of their recently murdered king, Laios, and the hand of the queen in marriage.

In the course of Sophocles' drama Oedipus discovers that he is actually the son of Laios, who was the unknown man at the crossroads, and Jokasta, who is now his own wife. Although this aspect of the story is not heavily emphasized in Sophocles' treatment, Oedipus has inherited his malignant doom from his father Laios, who (at least according to some versions of the myth) offended the gods and was warned by Apollo not to have any children. (This is mentioned, for example, by Aeschylus, *Seven Against Thebes* 742-52.) When *Oedipus at Colonus* alludes to the doom or curse that lies over the house of Oedipus (e.g. 369, 596, 965), this may be traced back not only to Oedipus' own deeds, but to those of his father before him. So too in *Antigone*, the doom on the house of Oedipus is clearly marked at the outset (1-6), and persists as a background theme of the play (49-60, 593-603, 856-71).

In *Oedipus the King*, when Oedipus discovers the dreadful truth about himself he puts out his own eyes in horror and longs only to go into exile from Thebes. Since he acted in ignorance and (in the case of the parricide) in self-defence, he would be found innocent in a court of law, ancient as well as modern. But legal guilt and innocence have little to do with the kind of horror aroused by such revelations. Despite his innocence, Oedipus is a polluted man—a tainted outcast who risks bringing divine retri-

---

8 Thebes, Corinth and Delphi are identified on the map on p. viii.

bution not only on himself, but on all who associate with him. At the end of *Oedipus the King* his fate is left uncertain. He is dependent on Kreon, his brother-in-law and successor as king, who will not allow him to go into exile without first consulting Apollo's oracle at Delphi.

In the final scene of this play, the pathos of Oedipus' situation is enhanced by the presence of his two young daughters, Antigone and Ismene. Their age is not specified, but they are too young to understand rational advice from their father (1511). Oedipus tells Kreon to let his two adult sons look after themselves, but to take special care of his vulnerable girl-children, to whom he is very close (1459-66). He embraces them and bewails their lot, especially the disastrous effects of his behavior on their marriage prospects (1466-1502). Like most young children in tragedy, the girls do not speak, nor are they named or individuated, but they provide a touching dramatic tableau as they cling to their father. Oedipus begs Kreon to care for them as if he were their own father (1503-10), and tells them to pray for a happier life than his own (1511-14). Kreon never explicitly agrees to his brother-in-law's request, but he will be the girls' guardian in any case, now that Oedipus has fallen, since he is their uncle and the new head of the patriarchal family. If we are right in thinking this play followed the production of *Antigone* by a number of years, then we may assume that Sophocles expects us to remember that Kreon actually killed Antigone in the play named for her.

Some twenty years after *Oedipus the King*, Sophocles, by now an old man himself, returned to complete the story of Oedipus in his last play, *Oedipus at Colonus*. At the start of this play Oedipus has been wandering in exile from Thebes for many years, with only Antigone as his guide, companion and protector. Ismene has been supporting them with visits and news from Thebes. The sons of Oedipus, Eteokles and Polyneices, have come to blows over the right to rule in Thebes, and a great battle is impending. Oedipus is furiously angry with his sons, because, by contrast with his daughters, they first permitted his exile (427-30) and then did nothing to alleviate it (337-56). But an oracle has decreed that whoever has his support will win the throne of Thebes. Polyneices, who has assembled an army of six allies (known, along with him, as the "Seven against Thebes"), visits his father to request such support. But Oedipus is unrelenting. He curses his sons with a terrible fate: they will die at each other's hand in a battle over the throne of Thebes.

Although Oedipus himself is an old man in *Oedipus at Colonus*, his daughters are portrayed as still young girls. At the same time Kreon tactlessly implies (*OC* 751-2) that Antigone is rather beyond the proper age for marriage (about fifteen for girls in the Athens of Sophocles' time). We should not try too hard, however, to reconcile the ages of the characters in these plays. More significant is the emphasis on the many years that Oedipus has wandered, and on his old age, the effects of which have been enhanced by his terrible sufferings, in contrast to the youthfulness of his children. Likewise in *Antigone*, Kreon is represented as an adult man in contrast to the youthfulness of Antigone, Ismene and Haimon on the one hand, and the old age of the messenger, the chorus and Teiresias on the other.

The latest of the three dramas points back to the events of *Oedipus the King*, but also forward (in mythic time) to the earliest of the three. Even though Antigone's role is relatively minor in *Oedipus at Colonus*, her character recalls her portrayal in *Antigone*, especially in contrast to Ismene (cf. esp. *OC* 1724-36). Sophocles clearly hoped that at least some of his audience would remember the contrast between the impetuous, transgressive Antigone and her "good girl" sister. Moreover Polyneices explicitly asks his sister bury him (*OC* 1405-13), and her final request to Theseus, king of Athens, is that she be allowed to return to Thebes for this purpose (1769-72).

When *Antigone* itself opens, Oedipus has died. The great battle between the Thebans, led by Eteokles, against Polyneices and his many allies, has just ended in victory for Thebes. The two brothers are dead at each other's hand, and Kreon, their uncle, is in power. As Antigone reveals in the prologue, Kreon has commanded an honorific burial for Eteokles, the defender, but forbidden burial entirely to Polyneices (for the significance of this see Essay p. 77-8). The emphasis here is quite different from other treatments of this part of the story that we know about. There is virtually no mention in earlier versions either of Kreon's specific prohibition or of Antigone's defiance (though our lack of evidence does not prove there were no such tales). In most accounts, Kreon forbids burial to Polyneices' entire army, and eventually backs down under the influence of Theseus, king of Athens. Sophocles may have been the first to shift the emphasis away from the unburied Argive army (merely touched on by Teiresias in lines 1080-84) towards the special case of Polyneices.

There is one possible exception to this. At the end of Aeschylus' tragedy *Seven Against Thebes* (produced in 467 BCE), the corpses of both brothers are brought in, and both Antigone and Ismene are in attendance as mourners. A herald proclaims Kreon's edict forbidding the burial of Polyneices, and Antigone declares her intention to defy it, alone if necessary. This scene is extremely close to Sophocles' play, but there are some interesting differences as well. In the Aeschylean version, the punishment for disobedience is not specified as death, nor is Antigone as isolated as she is in our play, for the chorus of Theban young women is divided in their sympathies. Accordingly, half of them go with Antigone to bury Polyneices, while the other half follow the official funeral cortège of Eteokles (presumably accompanied by Ismene).

There is a complication, however, in viewing *Seven Against Thebes* as part of the literary and mythic background for *Antigone*. Many scholars believe that the end of *Seven* was composed later, *after* Sophocles' *Antigone*, in order to cohere more neatly with that play in later revivals. If this is the case, then we have virtually no evidence concerning Antigone prior to Sophocles. But we do know that Antigone's own death was not an unalterable aspect of the myth, since Euripides composed a play (now lost) in which she survived, married Haimon, and bore him a son. We also know that Haimon played a different role in other versions: in the lost epic he was a victim of the Sphinx. Sophocles may also have enhanced the role of Ismene and invented that of Eurydike, Kreon's wife. So even if Kreon's edict were an established part of the tradition, the audience of Sophocles' play would not have been certain of the outcome for the central characters. The dramatist seems to have shaped the mythic materials in such a way as to emphasize personal conflict, blood-kinship and gender issues.

ANTIGONE

CHARACTERS

ANTIGONE, daughter of Oedipus (former king of Thebes)
ISMENE, daughter of Oedipus
CHORUS, fifteen aged noblemen of Thebes
KREON, king of Thebes, uncle and guardian of Antigone and Ismene
GUARD, an aged and lowly soldier under Kreon's command
HAIMON, son of Kreon
TEIRESIAS, an aged prophet
MESSENGER, an attendant of Kreon
EURYDIKE, wife of Kreon
Guards and attendants of Kreon, Teiresias and Eurydike

[Setting: Outside the royal palace of Thebes. The scene shows the façade of the palace, which has a large central door. The time is just before dawn, on the morning following the successful defeat of Polyneices and his allies in their assault on Thebes.]

[Enter Antigone and Ismene from the palace.]

ANTIGONE
Ismene, my own sister, sharing the self-same blood,
of all the evils that descend from Oedipus
do you know one that Zeus does not fulfill for us,
the two still living?[1] There is nothing—no!—no grief,
no doom, dishonor or disgrace that I've not seen   5
counted among the evils that are yours and mine.[2]
Now this! What is this proclamation that they say

---

1 The dead Oedipus belonged to a cursed family, and his children have inherited his misfortunes. (For the mythic background above, p. 13-18.) Zeus is mentioned as the king of the gods, who is concerned with crime and punishment from one generation to the next.

2 In *Oedipus at Colonus*, Antigone and Ismene are portrayed as suffering many hardships after their father's exile. Cf. also *Oedipus the King* 1486-1502.

the general has just made to all the city's people?[1]
Have you heard anything? Or are you unaware
that evils due to enemies approach our friends?[2]   10

ISMENE

To me no word of friends has come, Antigone,
sweet or distressing, since the time when you and I
were both deprived, we two, of our two brothers, both
struck dead by two-fold hand within a single day;
and since the army of the Argives disappeared   15
during the night just past, I have learned nothing new—
whether my fortune has improved or I am doomed.

ANTIGONE

I knew it well. That's why I summoned you outside
the courtyard gates, for you to hear me by yourself.

ISMENE

What is it? You are clearly brooding on some news.   20

ANTIGONE

What? Has not Kreon honored only one of our
two brothers with a tomb, and dishonored the other?[3]
Eteokles he has seen fit to treat with justice, so
they say, and lawfully[4] concealed beneath
the ground, there to be honored by the dead below;   25
but as for Polyneices' miserable corpse,
they say the townsfolk have received a proclamation,
that none may shroud him in a tomb or wail for him;

1 The "general" is Kreon, who has been made commander-in-chief as well as
king of Thebes by the death of Eteokles and Polyneices. He also displays a
military outlook in his capacity as king and father (see especially 639-80 and
cf. e.g. 241, 1033-4).

 "City" translates the Greek word *polis*. The *polis* or city state was the largest political unit of classical Greece. It included not just the city proper, but the
surrounding rural lands and villages.

2 This line could mean "the evils inflicted on our (recently-vanquished) enemies,"
or "the evils appropriate to enemies (generally)," or "evils coming from our
enemies (i.e. Kreon)." But however it is interpreted, it accords with the Greek
code of popular ethics that required one to help one's friends and harm one's
enemies, to which all the characters in the play adhere (see Essay p. 76-7 and
Blundell 1989).

3 The rituals of burial were enormously important in the Greek world. On the
issue in this play see further Essay p. 77-8.

4 This is the first occurrence of a key word in the play, *nomos*. It has been translated throughout as "law," but unlike the English word, *nomos* covers not only
the written laws of a society, but also custom and tradition, including the "unwritten laws" to which Antigone will later appeal (450-57).

he must be left unwept, unburied, treasure sweet
for watching birds to feed on at their pleasure.   30
They say that this is what good Kreon has proclaimed
for you and me—yes *me* as well!—and that he's coming
here to make his proclamation clear to those
who do not know;[1] nor does he view the matter as
a trivial one: the penalty prescribed for doing   35
this is death from stoning by the city's people.
That's how things stand; soon you'll reveal if you're
by nature nobly-born, or evil from good stock.

ISMENE

If that is how things are, unhappy one, what good
can *I* do, loosening or tightening the knot?[2]   40

ANTIGONE

See if you'll join in laboring to do a deed.

ISMENE

What deed of danger? What can you be thinking of?

ANTIGONE

See if you'll join these hands of mine to lift the corpse.

ISMENE

What, bury him? When it's forbidden to the city?[3]

ANTIGONE

Yes, bury my own brother—and yours too—if you're   45
not willing. *I* will not be caught in treachery.[4]

ISMENE

Audacious one! Against Kreon's express command?

ANTIGONE

He has no business keeping me from what is mine.

ISMENE

Alas! Just think, my sister, of our father—how
he perished, hated and in ill-repute, for errors   50
he himself detected, after he himself

---

1 The first proclamation was presumably made on the battlefield. Kreon's entrance speech will be an official proclamation to the city as a whole, as represented by the elders of the chorus.

2 A proverbial expression of helplessness in face of an insolubly knotty situation.

3 This could mean "by the city," in which case Ismene is equating Kreon with
   the city as a whole (cf. 79, 905).

4 Antigone means that she will never betray Polyneices, but from Kreon's point
   of view she will indeed be "caught in treachery."

gouged out his two-fold eyes with self-inflicting hand;[1]
next how his mother-wife—a two-fold name in one—
blighted her life with woven strands of twisted rope;[2]
third, our two brothers in a single day both killed   55
themselves in one another—wretched pair!—inflicting
one shared doom with two reciprocating hands;
look now in turn at us two, left here all alone—
our death will be the worst by far, if we defy
the law, and go beyond the power and vote of kings.[3]   60
We must remember, first, that we two are by nature
women and not fit to fight with men; second,
that we are ruled by others stronger than ourselves,
and so must bow to this and even greater griefs.[4]
So I for one shall beg those underneath the earth   65
to pardon me, since I am overpowered by force;[5]
I shall obey those who are in authority,
for deeds that are excessive make no sense at all.

ANTIGONE

I would not urge you otherwise, nor would it bring
me pleasure if you did now wish to act with me.   70
You be as you think best, but I shall bury him.
To me it's fine to die performing such a deed.[6]
I'll lie there, dear to him, with my dear friend,[7] when I've

---

1 Sophocles here appears to use a version of the story in which Oedipus stayed
   at Thebes (rather than being exiled) after blinding himself, and died there
   (though "perished" might simply mean "was ruined"). In *Oedipus at Colonus*,
   he dies at Athens with divine favor.

2 I.e. she hanged herself (cf. *Oedipus the King* 1263-4).

3 In myth and legend, most cities are governed by autocratic kings, who may be
   either tyrannical or benign. Tragedy often uses the language of kingship neu-
   trally. But the democratic Athenians were hostile to monarchy, and references
   to kingship in drama may have pejorative overtones. The word "vote" has
   democratic associations which produce a jarring effect when juxtaposed with
   the word "king," especially in this autocratic context (cf. also 633).

4 The idea that whoever is stronger either has the right to rule, or must in fact
   rule, is common in fifth-century Greek texts, and is associated with the influence of the sophists (above p. 4-5). But it would seem appropriately "feminine" in this context.

5 The plural ("those down beneath the earth") may include the gods of the underworld as well as Polyneices and Antigone's other dead family members.

6 "Fine" translates *kalos*, a powerful evaluative term with moral, aesthetic, heroic and aristocratic overtones (also used at 372, 723, 925).

7 "Dear" translates the word *philos* which means both "friend" and "dear," and
   often also "kin" (since family members are presumed to be "friends"). Here
   and elsewhere Antigone uses the language of friendship to express her deep

performed this crime of piety; for I must please
those down below a longer time than those up here,   75
since I shall lie there always. You, though, if you think
it best, dishonor what is honored by the gods.

ISMENE

I don't dishonor him; but it's impossible
for me by nature to defy the citizens.[1]

ANTIGONE

Make your excuses! *I* shall go and heap up earth   80
into a tomb to bury him, my dearest brother.

ISMENE

Alas! How I am filled with dread for you, poor wretch!

ANTIGONE

Don't fear for *me*; guide your own destiny aright.[2]

ISMENE

At least be sure that you reveal this deed to no
one else; conceal it secretly. I'll join in that.   85

ANTIGONE

Alas! Speak out! You'll be more hateful still if you
stay silent. No, proclaim my plan out loud to all!

ISMENE

You have a heart within you hot for chilling deeds.

ANTIGONE

I know that I am pleasing those I should please most.

ISMENE

Perhaps; but you're in love with the impossible.   90

ANTIGONE

Then when I've used up all my strength, I shall have done.

---

commitment to family loyalty (see Essay p. 76-7). But the passage also has an
incestuous coloring that hints at the perverted relationships in this particular
family, and at Antigone's later preference for her brother over a husband (905-
14).

1   The word translated here and elsewhere as "impossible" (*amēchanos*), is a significant one. It can be used actively, as here, to mean "lacking resources or
devices," or passively, to mean "intractable, unmanageable, inaccessible to any
resource or device" (90, 92, 363).

2   The word translated "destiny" (*potmos*) refers to the hand we are dealt by fate,
which should be used as well as possible. It does not imply predestination or a
rigid determinism. The word translated "aright" (*orthos*, meaning "straight,"
"upright," or "correct"), is a key word in the play, especially for Kreon (163,
167, 190, 403, 494, 675; cf. also 99, 636, 686, 706, 994, 1158, 1178, 1195 and see
Essay p. 82, 104). Besides "aright," I have translated it as "right," "rightly," or
"upright."

ISMENE

One should not hunt for the impossible at all.

ANTIGONE

If you speak so, you'll be a hateful enemy
to me, and justly hated by the dead man too.
Let me and the ill counsel that derives from me   95
suffer this awful fate; what I shall suffer will
be far less dire than dying an ignoble death!

ISMENE

Go, if you think it best; know that you're senseless to
be going, and yet rightly to your dear friends dear.[1]

[Exit Antigone along the side-entrance representing the path to the upland plain where the battle took place and Polyneices' body lies. Exit Ismene into the palace. Enter the chorus of fifteen old, white-haired noblemen of Thebes, singing and dancing. They enter along the other side-entrance, which represents the road from the city of Thebes proper.[2]]

CHORUS

Oh bright beam of the sun,[3]   *Strophe A*
loveliest light that ever shone   101
on seven-gated Thebes,[4]
at last you have appeared,
oh eye of golden day,
rising on Dirce's streams,[5]   105
stirring to headlong flight
with sharply piercing bit

---

1 The Greek word (*philos*) is both active and passive, covering "dear" as well as "friend," so Ismene's words are ambiguous between "rightly showing friendship to your friends/dear ones" and "rightly dear to your friends/dear ones" (cf. n. on 73).

2 Like most songs in tragedy, the chorus' entry song or *parodos* consists of a series of metrically equivalent pairs of stanzas, each pair consisting of a strophe and answering antistrophe. Here there are just two strophic pairs, and each strophe and antistrophe is followed by seven lines of anapests, a regular "marching" rhythm often used for choral entries or to mark the entrance of a character (cf. 376-83, 526-30, 626-30, 801-5). They are also used to accompany Antigone's final exit to her death (929-43).

3 The chorus invoke the newly risen sun in thanksgiving for the previous day's victory over the army of Polyneices and the Argives. Light is a common metaphor for escape from threatened disaster.

4 Thebes was famous for its seven gates. In his assault on the city, Polyneices brought six leaders, each of whom attacked one of the gates while Eteokles and his six allies defended them.

5 Dirce was a river to the west of Thebes, often used to symbolize the city.

the Argive, <u>shielded in white</u>,
in all his panoply, gone.[1]

Polyneices, roused by a double-edged
dispute,[2] led him to attack our land;   110
over our land he flew with a piercing
scream like an eagle, covering us with a
<u>*snow white wing*</u>,[3]
he with his numerous weapons and helmets   115
crested with horse-hair.

noble, arrogant but murderus

Over our halls he hovered,   *Antistrophe A*
maw gaping wide,[4]
<u>murderous</u> spears encircling
our city's seven-mouthed gates,   120
but was gone before he could glut
his jaws with our streaming blood,
or pine-fed Hephaistos could consume
our crowning wreath of towers[5] —
such a crashing of Ares surged at their backs,[6]   125
tough task for the dragon who wrestled him.[7]

For Zeus exceedingly hates the boasts
of a mighty tongue.[8] When he saw those men
coming on in a copious flood,
with the supercilious clanging of gold,   130
he struck one down with brandished fire
a man at his topmost goal, who rushed

---

1 This "warrior" represents the Argive army as a whole, not Polyneices or any individual fighter. The Argive shields are either painted white, or brightly shining. (The text is corrupt here, but this is the general sense.)

2 "Double-edged" means "disputatious," but also indicates that the brothers' quarrel was mutual, and suggests that there may have been fault on both sides.

3 This refers to the white or (bright) Argive shield (cf. 107).

4 The antistrophe continues the strophe's striking blending of monstrous eagle and battle imagery.

5 Hephaistos, the blacksmith god, is also god of fire, and here stands for fire itself. He is "pine-fed" because torches were made of pine wood.

6 Here, as often, the name of Ares the war god is used to stand for war itself (cf. 952).

7 The "dragon" stands for the Thebans, who originated from dragon's teeth sown in the ground by their founder Kadmos. The dragon's "wrestling foe" is the Argive eagle.

8 This is a variation on the theme of "mighty words" or "mighty thoughts," common Greek expressions for arrogant words (cf. 478-9, 768-9, 1351).

to raise up the victory cry.[1]

He teetered and fell to the resistant earth,	*Strophe B*
the fire-bringer who rushed madly on,	135
breathing on us, in frenzied Bacchanal,	
blasts of most hateful winds of enmity.[2]	
But he failed in his attempt; mighty Ares,	
our right-hand trace-horse,[3] struck down hard,	
dispensing other deaths to other men.	140

Seven captains at seven gates,
seven matched with an equal number,
left bronze tribute for Zeus, battle-turner.[4]
But that abhorrent pair of brothers,[5]
born from a single father and mother,   145
fixed two powerful spears in each other,
and both have their share in a double death.

But Victory of mighty name has come,	*Antistrophe B*
with joy responding to the joy	
of many-charioted Thebes.[6]	150
Now war is past, bring on forgetfulness!	
Let us visit all the temples of the gods	
with night-long dance and song!	

---

1   This is Kapaneus, one of Polyneices' allies. When he reached the top of the ramparts Zeus struck him down with lightning for his arrogance. This incident is used to typify the presumption as well as the punishment of the whole enterprise.

2   Kapaneus is likened both to a storm and to a Bacchant, one of the frenzied torch-bearing worshipers of Dionysos (who is also called Bacchus, as at 154). Besides being the god of wine and drama, Dionysos was an important patron god of Thebes, his birthplace.

3   In a four-horse chariot race, the trace-horse (i.e. the horse on the outside right) did the most work, because it had to run furthest at the turns. The metaphor indicates that Ares, the god of war, took an exceptional part in the battle and caused it to turn in favor of the Thebans.

4   It was customary after a victory to pile up the defeated enemy's armor and weapons as a thank-offering to a god, in this case Zeus in his capacity as "turner of battles" (*tropaios*, the word that gives us "trophy").

5   Eteokles and Polyneices, described with language that emphasizes the horror of their mutual fratricide.

6   Victory was worshiped as a goddess, often winged, and sometimes identified with Athena. She had a small but prominent temple on the Athenian Acropolis. Her joy "responds" to that of Thebes because it forms part of the reciprocal exchange of pleasures and favors between mortals and gods that is the basis of Greek religion.

May Bacchus, shaker of Thebes, lead on![1]

But here comes Kreon, the son of Menoikeus,   155
king of the land, and our new ruler since
this new fortune has come from the gods.[2]
What plan is he plying?[3]
Why has he called for a special assembly
of elders to meet here,[4]   160
sending a shared proclamation to all?

[Enter Kreon, along the side-entrance leading from the battlefield. He may still be wearing armor, and is accompanied by armed men. The parodos ends, and the meter returns to the iambic trimeters used for spoken dialogue.]

KREON
Oh men, the gods who tossed our city's ship on mighty
waves have safely righted it once more.[5] And so
I sent my messengers to summon you to come
away from all the rest, because I know you always   165
did revere the power of Laios' throne;[6] so too
when it was Oedipus who steered the city right;
and when he perished, you remained still loyal to
their children, steadfast in your purpose and your thoughts.
So, since his sons have perished in a single day,   170
two brothers by a two-fold fate, both striking and

---

1 Bacchus (Dionysos), the patron god of Thebes, was often worshiped at night. Through the gift of wine he provides happy "forgetfulness" of human cares. Here, as often, he is envisaged as leading the dance in his own honor. He "shakes" Thebes with the thunder of dancing feet, but the image also foreshadows his role as the destructive purifier of the city (cf. 1115-54).

2 Kreon has become king only now that Eteokles and Polyneices are both dead. The emphasis on his newness warns us that he may be inexperienced and rash.

3 The verb literally means to row or "ply an oar," but is often used metaphorically for vigorous activity. Such maritime imagery is common among the Greeks (a sea-faring people).

4 Some of the language here echoes Athenian democratic terminology.

5 The metaphor of the ship of state, which already occurs in earlier texts, reappears at 189-90, and indirectly at 715-17 (cf. also n. on 158).

6 Note that the chorus are not a representative group of citizens, but a hand-picked group of elders loyal to the royal house. "Reverence" (Greek *eusebeia*) and related words are common in this play, and cover a wide range of obligations, including religious piety (e.g. 304, 778, 922-4, 1349-50) and various forms of respect for human beings, such as family members (e.g. 511), authority figures (e.g. 744), and others (e.g. 730). These forms of "reverence" may sometimes conflict (cf. n. 872).

struck down, hands foully stained with mutual fratricide,[1]
It's I who now hold all the power and the throne,
through my close bond of kinship to the perished dead.
    It is impossible to learn in full the spirit   175
of a man, his purpose or his judgment, till
he's shown up by experience of rule and law.[2]
For anyone who rules the city as a whole
and does not hold on to the counsels that are best,
but keeps a lock fixed on his tongue because of fear,[3]   180
I think that man most evil, and I always have;
and he who counts a friend as more important than
his fatherland, he's nowhere in my reckoning.
For I—bear witness Zeus, who sees all things always!—
I'd not keep silent if I saw some doom instead   185
of safety moving on the people of this town;
nor would I ever count a man as my own friend
who felt ill will towards this land; I recognize
that this ship keeps us safe, and only when we sail
upon it upright can we make friends for ourselves.   190
    Such are the laws with which I make this city great.
And brother to them is my proclamation to
the townsfolk in regard to Oedipus's sons.[4]
Eteokles, who perished fighting for this city,
and did all deeds of greatness with his spear, will be   195
concealed within a tomb with all the offerings
that go down to the greatest of the dead below.[5]
But his blood-kin, his brother—I mean Polyneices
who came back from exile with intent to burn
with fire from top to bottom his own fatherland   200
and his own family gods,[6] intent to gorge himself

---

1 Killing of one's own kin brought an exceptionally terrible stain of religious pollution (cf. above p. 15).

2 Kreon is aware that as a new king he must win his people's loyalty not only by the claim of birth but by his performance as a ruler (see further Essay p. 82).

3 A leader might fear, for example, the consequences of unpopular policies (like Kreon's own). But it is usually subjects rather than rulers who keep their tongues "locked out of fear" (cf. 505). The statement thus strikingly exemplifies Kreon's inappropriate application of truisms (see Essay p. 82).

4 The use of "brother" to mean "closely allied" is not exceptional in Greek, but it has special resonance here because of the subject of the play.

5 An honorable burial included ritual lamentation and offerings to the dead, especially libations, i.e. poured liquids, which literally "go down to the dead below." Libations might be of honey, milk, water, wine or olive oil. Other offerings included flowers, wreaths of wool, and locks of hair from the next of kin.

6 I.e. the temples of the gods of Thebes, worshiped by his family (cf. 284-7).

on blood he shared,[1] and make his countrymen his slaves—
this city has received a proclamation, not
to honor him with funeral rites or wail for him,
but all must leave his body unentombed, to be   205
the food of birds and dogs, an outrage to behold.
Such is my purpose; never shall evil men be held
in higher honor than the just, at least by me;
but he who bears good will towards this city will
be honored by me equally in life and death.   210

CHORUS
It pleases you, Menoikeus' son, to treat like this
the man who shows ill-will towards this city and
the kindly one. You have the power to use what law
you like regarding both the dead and us who live.

KREON
See to it, then, that you watch over what I've said.   215

CHORUS
Assign this burden to some younger man to bear.

KREON
There are already watchers set to guard the corpse.

CHORUS
What else besides that would you order us to do?

KREON
Not to collaborate with those who disobey.

CHORUS
No one's so foolish as to be in love with death.   220

KREON
That is indeed the payment: death. But all the same,
profit destroys men often, through the hope of gain.[2]

*[Enter Guard, an old man dressed as a lowly soldier. He enters slowly and
hesitantly along the side-entrance leading from the battlefield.[3]]*

GUARD
My lord, I really cannot say that I've arrived
here out of breath with speed or light and fleet of foot.

---

1 Primarily the blood of his brother Eteokles, but also of the Thebans generally
   (his broader kin).

2 On "hope" see Essay p. 91; on Kreon's imagery see Essay p. 82.

3 In "real" time, Antigone could not have buried the corpse by now. But the
   intervening speeches, and especially the choral song, here as often mark the
   passage of an indeterminate period sufficient for dramatic purposes.

No, many times my anxious thoughts brought me up short,   225
and made me wheel round in the road to travel back.
My spirit spoke to me loquaciously, like this:[1]
"Poor fool, why go where you will pay the penalty?"
"Stopping again, you wretch? If Kreon hears about
this from some other man, you're bound to suffer grief!"   230
These ruminations made my progress leisurely
and slow, until a short road turned into a long.[2]
But in the end, the plan of coming to you won,
and if my words mean nothing,[3] I'll speak anyway.
For I have come here holding firmly to the hope   235
that I can suffer nothing that is not my fate.[4]

KREON

What is the reason for this apprehensiveness?

GUARD

I want to tell you my own situation first.
I did not do the deed, or see the one who did,
and it would be unjust for me to come to harm.   240

KREON

You're aiming well and building fences round the deed.[5]
It's clear you've something unexpected to reveal.

GUARD

Great hesitation is induced by awful things.

KREON

Won't you speak out at last, and then get out of here?

GUARD

All right, I'm telling you. The corpse—someone just now   245
has buried it and gone; they sprinkled thirsty dust
upon its skin and carried out the proper rites.

---

1 Personal uncertainty is often represented in Greek as a dialogue between a
   speaker and his or her mind or spirit (cf. 376 and the English idioms "a divided mind" and "in two minds"). The guard's "spirit" argues both sides of
   the case with him.

2 In a metatheatrical moment, the guard's words draw attention to his leisurely
   progress down the long entry ramp (*eisodos*).

3 This phrase apparently means that since the doer of the deed is unknown, the
   guard's narrative will be useless. But it could also conceivably mean "if I speak
   my own death-warrant."

4 This is not a claim about fate and free will, but a cliché equivalent to "que sera
   sera." On fate and human responsibility see Essay p. 103.

5 The guard's preamble is a "fence" of words to protect himself from blame.
   "You're aiming well" may mean that he is on target in his fears for the future,
   or that he is protecting himself from behind his "fence."

KREON

What are you saying? What man dared to do this deed?[1]

GUARD

I do not know. There was no mark from pick-axe blows,
no earth thrown up by mattocks;[2] no, the ground was hard   250
and dry, not broken up or furrowed by the weight
of wagon wheels. The doer was one who left no sign.[3]
When our first watcher for the day pointed this out,
uncomfortable amazement came upon us all.[4]
The corpse had disappeared—not buried in a grave,   255
but covered with light dust as if to deflect a curse.[5]
No sign was visible that any dog or savage
animal had been there tearing at the corpse.[6]
Abusive words began to rumble back and forth,
with guard accusing guard, and in the end we would   260
have come to blows—no one was there to hinder it.
For each and every one of us had done the deed,
but no one clearly so,[7] and all pled ignorance.
We were prepared to take up red-hot iron in
our hands,[8] to walk through fire, to swear oaths by the gods   265
that we had not done this ourselves, and had no knowledge
of who else had planned or carried out the deed.
     When our inquiries got us nowhere, then at last
one man spoke up who made us all bow down our heads

---

1   Note Kreon's assumption that the doer must have been male (cf. 61-2, 221-2, 307, and Essay p. 88-9).

2   A mattock is a large heavy hoe, used to break the ground for farming.

3   This slightly mysterious phrase and the miraculous air of the whole description will prompt the chorus to suggest that the gods played a part in the burial (278-9).

4   Their astonishment is "uncomfortable" both because they are baffled and because they fear the consequences of their discovery.

5   Anyone who passed an unburied corpse without covering it with dirt was considered cursed or "polluted," i.e. subject to a taint that would bring divine disapproval.

6   A light sprinkling sufficed for ritual purposes, but one would not expect this to deter scavenging animals (257-8). Despite this hint of divine preservation, which suits the dramatic moment (cf. 278-9), the text elsewhere suggests that Polyneices' body is in fact rotting and torn by wild animals (409-12, 1016-22, 1198, 1202; cf. 29-30, 205-6, 1080-83).

7   I.e. they all accused each other, but none of them had proof.

8   This recalls the medieval European "trial by fire," in which an innocent person could supposedly hold red-hot iron in the hand without injury. But there is no other evidence for such a custom among the ancient Greeks. "Walking through fire" is presumably a similar "test" of guilt or innocence.

towards the ground in fear; there was no way for us   270
either to contradict him or do as he said
and fare well from it. His advice was that this deed
should be reported to you rather than concealed.
This view won out, and I, ill-fated one, became
the one condemned by lot to win this fine reward.   275
I'm here against my will; against yours too, I know.
For no one likes a messenger who brings bad news.

CHORUS

My lord, my mind has been suggesting for some time
that possibly this deed was prompted by the gods.

KREON

Stop speaking now, before you stuff me full of rage,   280
or you'll be found to have no sense despite your age.[1]
The words you speak are unendurable—to think
divinities might be concerned about this corpse!
Did they conceal his body to bestow a special
honor on a benefactor—he who came   285
to burn their pillared temples and their offerings,
to scatter into pieces their own land and laws?
Do you see gods bestowing honor on the evil?
It cannot be! No, there are men who chafe at me
within the city, rumbling at me secretly   290
for some time now,[2] heads tossing, necks not justly held
beneath the yoke in due contentment with my rule.
I understand the situation well: the guards
were bribed by them with payment to perform this deed.
Money! No institution that's as evil ever   295
grew into existence for the human race.[3]
This wipes out cities, forces men to leave their homes,[4]
re-educates and warps the minds of mortals that
were good, inducing them to turn to shameful things,
shows human beings how to undertake all crimes,   300
and come to know impiety in every deed.
   Yet those who hired themselves for cash and did this deed

---

1 The old were expected to have the wisdom of their years (cf. n. on 735). To be
   simultaneously old and foolish was therefore doubly reprehensible.
2 I.e. the burial reflects the kind of dissatisfaction with Kreon that some of the
   citizens had voiced privately even before the decree.
3 The word translated "institution" (*nomisma*) is closely related to the word *nomos* (see n. on 24). In prose, it normally means "current coin" or "money."
4 Greed for money causes warfare (including civil strife), which in turn causes
   displacement and exile.

ensured that they would pay the penalty in time.
But by the reverence that Zeus receives from me,
know this full well—and I am speaking under oath: 305
if you guards do not find the one whose hand performed
this burial, and show him plainly to my eyes,
Hades won't be enough for you; before you die
you'll hang alive until you make this outrage clear,[1]
so that in future you may seize your plunder knowing   310
where to get your profits from, and learn that you
should not be fond of profiting from every source.
For you will see that after shameful takings the
majority of people end up doomed, not saved.

GUARD
Will you grant me a word, or shall I just turn and go?   315

KREON
Do you not know that even these words trouble me?

GUARD
But is their bite felt in your spirit or your ears?

KREON
Why try to pin down the location of my pain?

GUARD
The perpetrator pains your mind, but I your ears.

KREON
Oh what a natural chatterbox you are, it's clear!   320

GUARD
Perhaps; but I am not the one who did this deed.

KREON
You did the deed, and sold your life for money too.

GUARD
Ah!
How awful to believe when your beliefs are false!

KREON
Play with the word "belief."[2] But if you don't reveal

---

1   Hades, the god who rules the underworld, here (as often) stands for death.
    Kreon means that mere death will not be good enough for the guards, but they
    will die only after hanging up until they confess their guilt. The reference is
    not to death by hanging, but to a form of torture which might result in death.

2   Kreon is scoffing at the clever rhetorical wording of the guard's previous line.
    Such concepts as belief, opinion and knowledge were much discussed by phi-
    losophers interested in exploring the difference between appearance and real-
    ity, or belief and knowledge, and by rhetoricians whose art was designed to
    induce belief in the hearer.

the perpetrators of this deed to me, then you'll   325
admit that profits basely won bring suffering.

[Exit Kreon, into the palace.]

GUARD

Above all else may he be found. But whether he
is caught or not—that is for fortune to decide—
there's no way that you'll see me coming here again.
On this occasion I've been saved beyond my hope   330
and judgment, so I owe the gods great gratitude.

[Exit Guard, along the same side-entrance by which he arrived.]

CHORUS[1]

Awesome wonders are many,[2]   *Strophe A*
but none of them more awesome
than the human race.[3]
This creature travels the grey sea   335
before the stormy winter wind,
pressing through surging waves that crest about him;
the highest of gods he wears away,
the tireless immortal Earth,[4]
turning her with the offspring of horses,[5]   340
as the plow runs to and fro from year to year.

The tribe of light-headed birds,   *Antistrophe A*
all kinds of savage beasts,
and creatures born in the salty sea,
he traps with his intricate coiling nets   345
and leads away—ingenious man!

1 The chorus now dance and sing the first *stasimon* ("song in position"), which
   consists of two strophic pairs and is followed by eight lines of anapests (376-
   83). The starting point for their meditation on the nature of humanity is the
   extraordinary, almost miraculous feat of burial that the guard has just described.
   But the ode has far-reaching implications for many of the broader themes of
   the drama (see Essay p. 85-6).

2 The word translated "awesome" (*deinos*) is ambiguous between "clever," "won-
   derful" and "dreadful." Where the last meaning predominates, it has been translated "awful."

3 The Greek word here is *anthrōpos*, which means "human being" as opposed to
   "man." But later the word "man" (*anēr*) is used (346), reflecting the Greek tendency to regard the male as the norm and standard of humanity. The activities
   described are also those primarily associated with the male. It is therefore not
   inappropriate to use "he" as the subject of the verbs.

4 Earth does not rule the other gods, but she is "highest" because she is both
   oldest (age implies dignity) and the mother of all.

5 This probably refers to mules (offspring of horses and donkeys), which were normally used for ploughing. The taming of horses is mentioned in the antistrophe.

With devices he overpowers
the mountain-roaming beast
that dwells in the wilderness,
he breaks the shaggy-necked horse with a yoke   350
on its neck, and the tireless mountain bull.

Speech and wind-swift purpose,   *Strophe B*
these has he taught himself,
and the impulse to civic law,
and how to escape the shafts   355
of the inhospitable frosty sky
and the harsh shafts of the rain—
all-resourceful! Resourceless
he meets nothing the future holds.
Only from Hades will he fail   360
to find escape; and yet escape
from impossible sicknesses,
this he has devised

By means of skilful contrivance,   *Antistrophe B*
clever beyond hope,   365
he comes to evil sometimes,
sometimes to good.
When he weaves in the laws of the earth,
and the gods' sworn justice,[1]
he is high in his city;[2] citiless   370
is he whose daring makes him
join with what is not fine.
May he never share my hearth,
may I never share his thinking,
he who would do such things.   375

[Enter Guard leading Antigone, along the side-entrance by which he exited.
Antigone's eyes are cast down.[3]]

---

1 The "laws of the earth" suggest both human laws like Kreon's, and the laws of
   the underworld. "Weaves in" means that he maintains these laws as part of his
   life (but the text here is thought by many to be corrupt). "The gods' sworn
   justice" means justice that he has sworn by the gods to uphold.

2 The wording also suggests "his city stands high." Both meanings are particularly relevant to Kreon. "Citiless" in the next clause suggests not only that a
   wrongdoer may be exiled, but that a city composed of such people cannot
   stand firm. Note the close structural and verbal echo of 358, which falls in the
   same place in its strophe.

3 Again, the choral song has served to mark a considerable passage of time,
   during which Antigone has performed the "second burial" (see Essay p. 87).
   The next eight lines are in anapests, introducing the scene that follows.

My mind is divided! Is this a divine
portent?[1] I know her! How can I argue that
this girl here is not Antigone?
Unhappy one, and child of an unhappy
father, of Oedipus! What does this mean?   380
Surely they are not leading you *here,*
found disobeying the laws of the king,
caught in an act of foolishness?

GUARD

This is the woman who performed the deed. We caught
her in the act of burial. But where is Kreon?   385

[Enter Kreon from the palace, with attendants.]

CHORUS

He's here, returning opportunely from the house.

KREON

What chance event makes my arrival opportune?

GUARD

My lord, there's nothing mortals should forswear, since sworn
resolve is falsified by second thoughts. Take me:
I was insisting I would not be back here in   390
a hurry, after being stormed at with your threats.
But joy that we have prayed for past all hope surpasses
every other pleasure in extent; and so
I've come—despite the oaths I swore that I would not—
leading this girl here, who was caught performing rites   395
of burial. This time there was no drawing lots;
this lucky find belongs to me, and no one else.
Now take her, lord, yourself, as is your wish; you can
interrogate her and convict her; but it's just
that I should leave here fully free from all these evils.   400

KREON

This woman that you bring, where did you catch her? How?

GUARD

We caught her burying that man; now you know all.

KREON

Do you know what you're saying? Do you speak aright?

GUARD

I saw her burying the corpse to which you had
forbidden burial. Are these words clear enough?   405

---

1 The arrival of the royal princess under guard is so shocking to the chorus that
   they cannot believe their eyes, and suggest there must be a supernatural explanation (cf. 278).

KREON
And how was she observed and taken in the act?

GUARD
What happened was like this. When we got back to our
position, subject to those awful threats of yours,
we brushed off all the dust that had been covering
the body, stripping bare the putrifying corpse,   410
and sat down on the hilltop with the wind behind
us, to escape from being stricken by the stench,
each man alert, and rousing one another with
loud taunts at any who might slacken from the task.

    This lasted for the time it took the shining circle   415
of the sun to reach the center of the sky.
The heat was burning. Suddenly a whirlwind raised
a dusty column from the earth, a trouble high
as heaven, which filled up the plain, defacing all
the foliage of the trees, and choked the mighty sky.   420
We shut our eyes and bore the sickness sent by god.

    It took a long time for the storm to pass. And then
we saw this girl here wailing bitterly aloud,
in the piercing voice of a mother bird who sees her nest
is empty and her bed bereft of baby chicks.   425
Just so did she, on seeing that the corpse was bare,
cry out in lamentation, and call evil curses
down upon the ones who had performed this deed.[1]
At once she gathered thirsty dust with her bare hands,
and lifting high a brazen pitcher, finely-wrought,   430
she crowned the corpse by pouring three libation-streams.[2]

    The instant that we saw her, we rushed forward and
hunted her down; she was completely unperturbed;
We charged her with the deeds of burial, both this
one and the first, and she did not deny a thing—   435
a fact that brought me grief and pleasure both at once:
it is most sweet to have escaped from evils for
oneself; and yet to bring a friend to evil is
distressing.[3] But it's only natural that all

1 Note the echo of 384. The similarity in the descriptions of the two deeds underlines the similarity of Antigone's and Kreon's outlooks, and at the same
  time the diametrical opposition between their views.

2 Libations are liquids poured out in honor of the gods, or in this case, the dead
  (see n. on 197). The usual number was three.

3 The guard would not be a "friend" of Antigone's in our sense (cf. Essay p. 76-
  7), but as a servant of the family he wishes her well and feels an obligation of
  loyalty towards her (cf. the Messenger at 1192).

of this means less to me than my own safety.   440

KREON [to Antigone]
You there! You, bowing down your head towards the ground!
Do you admit it or deny you did the deed?

ANTIGONE
I don't deny it; I admit the deed was mine.

KREON [to the guard]
You may now take yourself away, wherever you
may wish, free and unburdened of this heavy charge.   445

[He turns back to Antigone.]

But as for you, tell me succinctly, not at length:
you knew a proclamation had forbidden this?

ANTIGONE
I knew. How could I not? It was a public fact.

KREON
And yet you had the daring to transgress these laws?

ANTIGONE
It was not Zeus who made this proclamation;   450
nor was it Justice dwelling with the gods below
who set in place such laws as these for humankind;[1]
nor did I think your proclamations had such strength
that, mortal as you are, you could outrun those laws
that are the gods', unwritten and unshakable.[2]   455
Their laws are not for now or yesterday, but live
forever; no one knows when first they came to light.
I was not going to pay the gods' just penalty
for breaking these, dreading the purposes of a
mere man. I knew that I must die—how could I not?—   460
regardless of the proclamation that you made.
But if I die before my time, I count that as
a profit. How can death not profit one who lives

---

1 Justice is often personified as sitting beside the throne of Zeus, king of the
   heavenly gods (e.g. *OC* 1382). But Antigone is appealing to Zeus not only as
   the supreme god of the sky, who is offended by the improper treatment of a
   corpse (cf. 1069-73), but also as ruler of the underworld (equivalent to Hades),
   the realm where Polyneices' body properly belongs. According to Antigone,
   there is a corresponding Justice who lives down below, representing the rights
   of the underworld divinities. On "earth" and "sky" gods see Essay p. 87-8.

2 "Unwritten laws" are customs and traditions, as opposed to codified law (see
   Essay p. 87). Kreon's proclamation is not in the usual sense a "written law,"
   but it is equated here with the laws of the state, which would generally be
   written down.

surrounded by as many evils as myself?
For me, therefore, to meet this doom is equal to   465
no grief at all. But if I had endured the son
of my own mother to lie dead without a grave,
that would have brought me grief; but I'm not grieved by *this*.
And if you think my present deeds are foolishness,
perhaps the one who calls me foolish is the fool.   470

CHORUS
The child shows clearly her fierce father's fierceness; but
she does not understand the way to yield to evils.

KREON
Know well that over-rigid purposes most often
fall; the iron that is most powerful, that has
been baked in fire until it is extremely hard,   475
you'll see most often shattered into little bits;
a slender curb, I know, will school the spirit of
a raging-tempered horse; it is impossible
to harbor mighty thoughts when you are someone's slave.
This girl knew well how to commit an act of outrage   480
when she first transgressed against the published laws;
and here's a second outrage: after doing it
to boast of it and laugh, exulting in her deed.
It's clear enough that I'm no man, but she's the man,
if she can get away with holding power like this.[1]   485
No, whether she's my sister's child, or tied to me
closer by blood than all my household under Zeus,[2]
she won't escape from a most evil doom, nor will
her sister, her blood-kin, the other whom I hold
equally guilty in the planning of this tomb.   490
Call her. Just now I saw her in a frenzy in
the house, no longer in possession of her mind.

[Two of Kreon's attendants exit into the palace.]

The heart of those contriving in the dark what is

---

1 Kreon reveals his own preoccupations by oddly describing Antigone's success
   with a word (*kratos*) normally used for political power (cf. e.g. 173, 873). On
   Kreon and gender see Essay, p. 88-9.

2 Literally, "than Zeus of the courtyard." This is one of the titles under which
   Zeus was worshiped as a guardian of the family. An altar to Zeus of the Hearth
   was placed in the central courtyard of the Greek house, where the whole household might gather for sacrifice. Kreon's form of expression makes it very clear
   that he is violating his obligation towards Zeus in this capacity. We may also
   recall that the "sister" he mentions is Jokasta, not only Antigone's mother but
   the incestuous mother-wife of Oedipus.

not right is often caught out in deceit before
they act. But this I also loathe—when someone caught   495
performing evil wants to glorify the deed.[1]

ANTIGONE

Take me away and kill me. Do you want more than this?

KREON

No more. If I have that, then I have everything.

ANTIGONE

Then what's delaying you? For there is nothing in
your words that's pleasing to me—may there never be!   500
And naturally you disapprove of mine as well.
Yet how could I have won more glorious renown
than by the act of placing my own brother in
a tomb? These people here would say my action pleases
all of them,[2] if fear did not lock up their tongues.   505
But this is one of kingship's many blessings—that
it can both act and speak just as it wishes to.

KREON

This view is yours alone of all these Kadmeans.[3]

ANTIGONE

It's their view too; because of you they curb their lips.

KREON

Aren't you ashamed of thinking differently from them?   510

ANTIGONE

I'm not ashamed of reverence for my flesh and blood.

KREON

Did he who died opposing him not share that blood?

ANTIGONE

He shared it, from one mother and one father too.

KREON

Then why give honor that's irreverent in his eyes?[4]

---

1 I.e. Ismene tried to conceal the deed, but has been betrayed by the unusual
   behavior resulting from her guilty conscience, whereas Antigone has been
   caught in the act and is not ashamed of it.

2 Antigone gestures towards the chorus. But the audience might also feel themselves to be included among "these people here."

3 "Kadmean" means "Theban," after Kadmos, the founder of Thebes.

4 Since the two brothers were enemies, Kreon expects the dead Eteokles to be
   angered by Antigone's respectful treatment of Polyneices.

ANTIGONE
The dead man's corpse will not bear witness to your words.[1]   515

KREON
Yes, if you honor the irreverent equally.

ANTIGONE
No, for it was his brother, not some slave, who died.

KREON
Died trying to sack this land, the other in defense.

ANTIGONE
Despite that, Hades longs to see these laws fulfilled.[2]

Gods call for burial

KREON
But good and bad should not share in them equally.   520

ANTIGONE
Who knows if this is not deemed faultless down below?[3]

KREON
An enemy is not a friend, even in death.

ANTIGONE
My nature joins in friendship, not in enmity.[4]

KREON
If you must show them friendship, go and do so down
below! But while I live a woman shall not rule.[5]   525

[The two attendants return from the palace leading Ismene. She is distraught.]

CHORUS
But here is Ismene in front of the gates,
pouring the tears of a loving sister;
a storm-cloud is hanging over her brow,
blighting her visage flushed with blood,
wetting her lovely cheek with rain.   530

KREON
You there, who lurked inside the house, a viper sucking

---

1   Antigone may mean that since Eteokles is dead he is not available as a witness, or that he will not take the view Kreon imputes to him.

2   These "laws" are the traditional rites of burial.

3   I.e. perhaps in death Eteokles will respect his brother's right to burial. Kreon's response, that enmity extends even beyond the grave, is more plausible in terms of traditional Greek attitudes.

4   In this line Antigone uses two unique words, which must have been carefully chosen (or coined) to express her essential nature. But her words should not be sentimentalized. For the Greeks, "friendship" with kin was a natural fact of birth, which should evoke loyalty regardless of personal sentiment (see Essay p. 76-7, 90).

5   This line is ambiguous. It could also mean "a woman shall not rule *me*."

out my blood without my knowledge—I was not
aware of nurturing two dooms to overthrow
my throne—come, tell me, will you too admit you helped
perform this burial, or swear your ignorance?   535

ISMENE

I did the deed—if she will join in saying so.
I share in bearing the responsibility.

ANTIGONE:

Justice will not allow this, since you did not want
to do it, nor did I give you a share in it.

ISMENE

But in these evils I am not ashamed to make   540
myself a fellow-sailor of your suffering.

ANTIGONE

Hades and those below know who can claim this deed;
I do not like a friend who loves in word alone.

ISMENE

Don't, sister! Don't dishonor me by keeping me
from joining in your death and rites for him who died.[1]   545

ANTIGONE

Don't try to share this death with me. Don't claim as yours
a deed you did not touch. My own death will suffice.

ISMENE

How can I long for life if you leave me behind?

ANTIGONE

Ask Kreon that; he is the one you care about.

ISMENE

Why give me pain like this, when it's no help to you?   550

ANTIGONE

If I do laugh at you then it's because of grief.[2]

ISMENE

How then may I attempt to help you, even now?

ANTIGONE

Just save yourself; I don't begrudge you your escape.

---

1 Ismene seems to think that by accepting blame for the burial she can also share the credit for it.

2 Mocking or gloating laughter was a standard way of expressing contempt for an enemy or avenging oneself for an injury (cf. 483, 647, 839-42, 1084-5). Antigone is retaliating against Ismene for the pain caused by her sister's failure to help her. Ismene's response shows an attempt to repair their relationship even now.

ISMENE
Wretch that I am! Must I miss sharing in your doom?

ANTIGONE
You must; you made the choice to live, and I to die.   555

ISMENE
But not without me trying to talk you out of it.

ANTIGONE
One side approved your thinking and the other mine.[1]

ISMENE
And yet the two of us are equally at fault.[2]

ANTIGONE
Take heart! You are alive, but my soul has long since
been dead, that I might offer help to those who died.   560

KREON
One of these two, I say, has just been shown to be
quite senseless, and the other's been that way since birth.

ISMENE
Yes, lord; in evil fortune even people's inborn
sense does not remain within them, but departs.

KREON
Like yours, when you chose evil deeds with evildoers.[3]   565

ISMENE
How can I live my life without her, all alone?

KREON
Her—do not speak of her as someone still alive.

ISMENE
But will you really kill your own child's bride-to-be?[4]

KREON
Yes; there are other plots of land for him to plow.[5]

1 On one "side" of this imaginary debate is Kreon, on the other the gods and the
   sisters' dead family members.

2 Presumably Ismene means that she is equally guilty because she sympathizes
   with Antigone's act. Or she may be referring to the fact that Kreon holds them
   equally responsible.

3 Kreon wilfully misinterprets Ismene's reference to the sisters' "evil fortune,"
   as if she meant bad behavior.

4 This is the first mention in the play of Haimon, Kreon's son. His betrothal to
   Antigone may have been invented by Sophocles (above, p 18). If so, Ismene's
   words will have been quite a dramatic surprise for the original audience.

5 I.e. other marriage partners are available to Haimon. Kreon here echoes the
   Athenian marriage ceremony, in which the wife was given to the husband "for
   the plowing of legitimate children." For his tone here see Essay p. 92.

ISMENE
Not like the harmony that fitted him to her.[1]   570

KREON
I hate for sons of mine to marry evil women, ← Antigone

ISMENE
Oh dearest Haimon, how your father dishonors you![2]

KREON
You're paining me too much, you and your marriage-bed.

ISMENE
Will you deprive him, your own offspring, of this girl?

KREON
It's Hades who will stop this marriage taking place.   575

ISMENE
It has been settled, so it seems, that she must die.

KREON
Settled—for you as well as me. No more delays!
Take them inside the house, attendants. From now on
they must be women and not wander unrestrained.[3]
For even people who are bold will try to find   580
escape when they see Hades closing on their life.

[Attendants take Antigone and Ismene back into the palace. Kreon remains on stage.[4]]

1 These words may suggest a special personal bond between the couple, in which case they express an unusual attitude towards marriage compared to most ancient Greek sources. But they may simply mean that the couple is well-matched dynastically.

2 Some commentators assign this line to Antigone rather than Ismene (to whom the manuscripts give it). Manuscripts do make such mistakes, but the arguments in favor of Antigone depend on a sentimental view of her relationship with Haimon, of which there is no other sign in the text. It would not be inappropriate for the affectionate Ismene to call Haimon "dearest." "Your marriage bed" in the next line is normal Greek idiom for "this marriage that you keep going on about."

3 According to Athenian norms, respectable women were supposed to leave the house as little as possible. But on the stage, where the scene is always outside, it was necessary for women to appear outside the house if they were to participate in the drama. The dramatists often play on this tension between social propriety and dramatic necessity (cf. 18-19, and Eurydike's explanation at 1183-5). Here Sophocles makes Antigone's freedom, necessary for dramatic purposes, into a further sign of her unruliness in Kreon's eyes.

4 It is usual in Greek tragedy for the actors to be absent during the choral songs. But Kreon seems to be present, perhaps for all the remaining songs of the play (cf. n. on 780).

CHORUS[1]

Blessed are they whose life has tasted no evil.	*Strophe A*
When a house is tossed by the gods,	
no aspect of doom is lacking;	
it spreads out over that family	585
like a surging wave of the salt sea	
running over the surface	
of murky darkness beneath;	
blown by tempestuous Thracian blasts	
it rolls black sand from the sea-bed,	590
and the wind-vexed headlands face	
its blows with a groaning roar.	

Ancient are the troubles I see	*Antistrophe A*
for the house of the Labdakids,[2]	
heaped on the troubles of the dead;	595
no new generation frees the family,	
but some god strikes them down	
and they find no release.	
Just now a light of hope shone forth	
from the last root of Oedipus' house;	600
but in its turn it is cut down	
by the bloody dust of the gods below,	
by senseless words and a Fury in the mind.[3]	

What transgression of men,	*Strophe B*
oh Zeus, can constrain your power?	605

1 The chorus now dance and sing the second *stasimon* (third choral song), which consists of two strophic pairs and is followed by five lines of anapests (626-30). In it they place the preceding events into the larger context of the inherited curse on the house of Oedipus. Like the previous song, it is most obviously relevant to Antigone but has broader implications extending to Kreon as well (see Essay p. 91-2).

2 The Labdakids are the descendants of Labdakos, who was father of Laios and grandfather of Oedipus.

3 The text is difficult here, and the imagery, as we have it, is very bold. Antigone and Ismene are the "last root" of their family, because they are the last means of propagating it. Light is a common metaphor for hope and safety in Greek (cf. 100-109), but here it does double duty by signifying the nurturing sunshine that might have helped the "root" to grow. The "bloody dust" alludes to the dust that Antigone sprinkled on her brother's corpse. This, along with her rash ("senseless") words to Kreon and her own frenzied behavior, is responsible for her demise. Furies are goddesses of vengeance, who exert their will by driving their victims to madness (most famously in the case of Orestes). This Fury represents divine vengeance manifested over the generations of the house of Oedipus. But Antigone is not the only one in this play who may be accused of "senseless words and a Fury in the mind" (cf. 1074-5).

Sleep that conquers all
cannot defeat it; nor can
the tireless months of the years.
A potentate unaged by time,
you occupy the dazzling   610
splendor of Olympus.
Both now and through the future,
as through the past, this law will stand:
no vast thing moves into mortal lives without doom.[1]

For widely-wandering hope   *Antistrophe B*
benefits many men; but many   616
it cheats with light-headed passions.[2]
it comes upon one who knows nothing
till he burns his foot in the hot fire.[3]
It was some clever person   620
who declared this famous saying:
evil seems good, sooner or later,
to someone whose mind
a god leads towards doom;
he fares but the briefest of time without doom.   625

[Enter Haimon, along the side-entrance leading from the city proper.]

Here is Haimon, the last and youngest-
born of your children. Has he arrived in
grief at the doom of his bride Antigone,
is he distraught to be cheated out of his
marriage-bed with his promised bride?[4]   630

KREON

We'll soon know better than a prophet could. My child,
have you come here in frenzy at your father, hearing
of my settled vote against your bride-to-be?
Or am I still your friend, whatever I may do?

---

1 This is an expression of the traditional Greek pessimistic view that great wealth
   and status lead human beings into disaster.

2 In Greek "hope" (*elpis*) is not always positive (Essay p. 91). "Passions" here are
   literally *erōtes*, the plural of *erōs*, passionate desire (cf. 781-800 and Essay p.93-
   94).

3 The image is probably of someone walking confidently over what appear to be
   cold ashes and accidentally stepping on a burning coal.

4 Lines 626-30 are in anapests, used once again to mark an important entrance.
   Note the formal symmetry of the encounter between Haimon and Kreon: four
   lines each, a pair of long speeches, each followed by two lines from the chorus
   leader, two lines each followed by stichomythia, and finally four lines each
   before Haimon exits.

HAIMON

Father, I'm yours. Your judgments, being good ones, guide   635
my path aright, and I shall follow where they lead;[1]
no marriage shall be reckoned by me as a prize
more valuable than having you as my good guide.

KREON

Just so, my child; that's how your heart should be disposed:
to stand behind your father's judgment in all things.[2]   640
This is the reason men pray to beget and keep
obedient offspring in their house—that they may pay
back evil to their father's enemies, and give
due honor to his friends, just as their father does.
But he who fathers children that provide no help,   645
what can you say he propagates but labors for
himself, and peals of laughter for his enemies?
So do not ever lose your senses, child, just out
of pleasure in a woman, knowing that an evil
woman as a bed-mate in your house will make   650
a chilly armful to embrace;[3] for what could be
a wound more serious than this, an evil friend?
So spit that girl away just like an enemy,
and let her marry someone else, in Hades' house.
For I have caught her disobeying openly,   655
this girl alone of all the city; and I shall
not falsify myself before the city, but
I'll kill her. Let her sing to Zeus of blood-kinship.[4]
For if I raise my relatives by birth to be
disorderly, outsiders will be even worse.   660
For he who is a good man in his household will
be shown to be a just man in the city too.
I have full confidence that such a man would both
rule well, and serve well as a subject under rule,

---

1 In Greek there is a subtle ambiguity in Haimon's words, between "I always
   follow your good judgment" and "*when* your judgment is good, I follow it."
   There is a similar ambiguity in the latter part of 638, which could mean "*when*
   you guide me well." Cf. also the ambiguity of "I'm yours" (635), which could
   mean "I am your son" or "I am loyal to you."

2 There is military metaphor here: Haimon is to be a dutiful soldier obeying his
   father's judgment.

3 Kreon's words ironically foreshadow Haimon's final embrace of Antigone
   (1236-7); compare also 653 with 1232.

4 This title alludes to Zeus's role as protector of the family (cf. 487 with note).

and in a storm of spears stand firmly in his place,   665
a just man and a good one at his comrades' side.
But that transgressor who does violence to the law,
or thinks to give commands to those who are in power,
whoever does this can receive no praise from me.
The one appointed by the city should be listened to,   670
in small things and in just things and the opposite.[1]
There is no greater evil than unruliness.[2]
It ruins cities and makes households desolate,
it breaks and turns to flight the ranks of allied spears.
But when the lives of mortals go aright, it is   675
obedience to rule that keeps most bodies safe.
Therefore we must defend the cause of order, and
by no means let a woman get the upper hand.
Better to fall, if we must do so, to a man;
then nobody could call us conquered by a woman.   680

CHORUS

To us, unless time's robbed us of our wits, you seem
to speak with sense about the things you're speaking of.

HAIMON

Father, the gods implant good sense in human beings,
the very best of everything that we possess.
I could not say—and may I never have the knowledge   685
to declare—that you're not right in what you say.
But things might also turn out well some other way.
It is my natural place to watch on your behalf,
at all that people say or do or criticize;
for awe at your expression hinders common men   690
from saying things that might displease you if you heard.
But I can hear, in dark obscurity, the things
the city says in lamentation for this girl:
that she among all women least deserves to die
the evillest of deaths for deeds most glorious,   695
since she did not let her own brother, fallen in
the bloody slaughter, lie unburied or be torn
apart by fierce flesh-eating dogs or birds of prey.
Is golden honor not the lot that she deserves?
Such murky rumors are advancing secretly.   700

---

1 The idea that in order to preserve civic order one must obey even unjust commands by a ruler accords with Kreon's generally military outlook. The thought is not uncommon in Greek texts, but it is often associated with slavery.

2 This is the first certain occurrence in Greek of the word *anarchia*, which gives us "anarchy." It means the collapse of rule and prevalence of disobedience.

My father, no possession is more valuable
to me than your good fortune; for what greater treasure
can a child have than a father thriving in
renown, or can a father have than such a son?
Do not, then, clothe yourself in just one attitude—   705
that what you say, and only what you say, is right.
For those who think that they alone possess good sense,
or that no other has a tongue or spirit such
as theirs, when opened up expose their emptiness.[1]
No, even if a man is clever, there's no shame   710
in learning many things and not straining too tight.
When trees beside a swollen winter torrent bend
and yield, you see how each twig is kept safe;
but those that strain against it perish root and branch.
And on a ship, if he who holds the power strains   715
the rigging tight and does not yield, he turns his rowing
benches over and completes his voyage upside down.[2]
So come, yield from your rage; allow yourself to change.
If there is judgment even in a younger person
like myself, I say it's best by far for men   720
to be by nature full of knowledge in all things.
If not—since things are not inclined to be that way—
it's also fine to learn from others who speak well.

CHORUS

It's fitting, lord, if he says something timely, that
you learn, and you from him, since both have spoken well.   725

KREON

Are men of my age to be taught to have good sense
by someone who has only grown to this man's age?

HAIMON

Only in what is just. And even if I'm young,
you should not look at someone's age, but at his deeds.

KREON

Revering the disorderly—at deeds like that?   730

HAIMON

I'd never urge you to revere an evildoer.

---

1 The image here may be that of a folded pair of writing tablets, which is opened
   up to find nothing written inside.

2 Haimon describes the ship's captain in a way that is applicable to a political ruler
   (cf. 738), and thus underlines the implications of the "ship of state" analogy.

KREON
And is this not the sickness *she's* afflicted with?

HAIMON
That's not what all the citizens of Thebes are saying.

KREON
And shall the city tell me what I should command?

HAIMON
You see how like a very young man that was said?[1]   735

KREON
Am I to rule this land at someone else's whim?

HAIMON
There's no true city that belongs to just one man.[2]

KREON
By law is not a city his who holds the power?

HAIMON
You'd do well ruling in a desert by yourself.

KREON
He's fighting as the woman's ally, so it seems.   740

HAIMON
If you're a woman; you're the one I care about.

KREON
Saying your father is unjust, most evil one?

HAIMON
Yes, since in justice I can see that you are wrong.

KREON
So I am wrong to show due reverence for my rule?

HAIMON
Irreverence, trampling on the honors of the gods.   745

KREON
Vile character, to give a woman precedence.

HAIMON
At least you will not catch me conquered by disgrace.

KREON
Yet all you say is spoken on behalf of *her*.

---

1 Young men were expected to be rash and hot-headed, in contrast to the greater dignity and restraint appropriate to maturity and the wisdom of old age (cf. 281, 726-7, 767).

2 A city governed by a monarch or "tyrant" might "belong to one man," but would not live up to the ideals of the Athenian democratic *polis*.

HAIMON
Of you and me as well, and of the lower gods.

KREON
There is no way that you will marry her alive!   750

HAIMON
Then she will die, in death destroying someone else!

KREON
Have you become so bold that you are threatening me?

HAIMON
What threat is it to speak against your empty judgments?

KREON
You'll weep for trying to teach me sense, when you have none.

HAIMON
If you were not my father, I'd say *you* lack sense.   755

KREON
Don't try to coax me with such words, you woman's slave.

HAIMON
You want to speak, yet hear no answer to your words?

KREON
What? By Olympus here above,[1] know well that you
will soon regret abusing me with your complaints.

[He addresses his attendants.]

Bring out that loathsome creature, so that she may die   760
at once, before her bridegroom's eyes, right at his side.

[Two attendants exit into the palace.]

HAIMON
No! No! She shall not perish at my side—do not
believe it! And you'll never see my face before
your eyes again; so you may rave on madly with
whatever friends still want to share your company!   765

[Haimon rushes from the stage along the side-entrance leading to the plain.]

CHORUS
My lord, the man has gone from us swift in his rage,
and grief lies heavy on the mind of one so young.

KREON
Let him be gone to do, or think, things greater than

---

1 Olympus stands for the sky (home of the "Heavenly" gods), to which Kreon
gestures as he swears by it (cf. Essay, p. 88).

52 SOPHOCLES

a man; he will not free those two girls from their doom.

CHORUS

Is your mind really set on killing both of them? _Ismene_   770

KREON

Not her who had no part in it; your words are good.

CHORUS

By what doom do you plan to kill the other one?

KREON

I'll lead her to a place deserted by the steps
of mortals, and conceal her, living, in a cave
dug from the rock, with just a little food, enough   775
to let the city as a whole escape pollution.[1]
And there perhaps by praying to the only god
that she reveres—Hades—she may be spared from death;
or else she'll come to recognize at last that to
revere the realm of Hades is excessive labor.[2]   780

CHORUS[3]

    Eros, unconquered in battle!   *Strophe*
    Eros, you plunder possessions,[4]
    you keep your night watch
    on a young girl's soft cheeks;

---

1 The Greek suggests not a natural cave but a chamber hollowed out of the rock
by human hands, with a passage cut into the mountain leading to the mouth
of the chamber itself (1215-17). Tombs of this kind have been found in Greece.
According to Kreon's original decree, the punishment was to be death by stoning (cf. 35-6). But since the perpetrator has turned out to be his kin, Kreon
attempts to avoid blood-pollution by letting Antigone die of "natural" causes
rather than killing her directly. Death by immurement was also felt to be appropriate to unmarried women, since it leaves the body concealed and
unpenetrated in death. Leaving some food in the cave is a further symbolic
evasion of responsibility and hence of pollution.

2 Commentators disagree over whether Kreon exits at this point. If he goes into
the palace, this would be the only time a male character besides the Messenger
enters or leaves the female realm, except for Kreon's own final exit (below, p.
75, n. 2). If he remains on stage throughout, that might help to explain the
chorus' lack of explicit support for Antigone. On the other hand, it seems strange
for him to wait throughout Antigone's long lament before sending her off to
her death at 885. If he does exit here, he returns at 882.

3 The chorus dance and sing the third *stasimon*, which consists of just one strophic pair. It is a hymn to Eros, god of passionate desire, to whom the chorus
attribute Haimon's behavior in the preceding scene. The short ode is followed
by five anapests introducing Antigone (801-5).

4 Eros destroys material goods, not only by making people spend recklessly, but
by provoking such destruction as the sack of Troy (caused by Paris's seduction
of Helen).

you range over the sea   785
and through wild rural dwellings;
not one of the immortals can escape you,
not one of us human beings
whose lives are but a day;[1]
and he who has you has madness.   790

You wrench aside minds to injustice,   *Antistrophe*
even of the just, to their ruin;
you have stirred up this quarrel too,
between men bound by blood;[2]
radiant desire is the victor,   795
shining in the eyes of the bride
who graces the marriage bed;[3]
this sits in rule by the mighty ordinances;[4]
for the game-playing goddess
Aphrodite is invincible in battle.   800

[Enter Antigone, led by guards from the palace.]

But now at this sight I myself am carried
away past the bounds of such ordinances,[5]
I can no longer hold back the streams
of my tears, when I see Antigone pass
to the bridal chamber where all must sleep.[6]   805

---

1   This is a common way of expressing the brevity of human life in contrast to the
    immortality of the gods (cf. 456-7).

2   The word translated as "bound by blood" (*xunaimos*, also at 198, 488, 659),
    echoes and puns on the name of Haimon. Related words for blood (*haima*) are
    used at 122, 202, 486, 512, 529, 976, 1022, 1175.

3   The eyes are often viewed as both a locus and a cause of erotic desire. The
    phrase is thus suggestive of erotic reciprocity, indicating the bride's own de-
    sire as well as her attractiveness to her bridegroom. But there has been no sign
    of such desire in Antigone.

4   The "mighty ordinances" are the moral laws sanctioned by the gods, like the
    "unwritten laws" to which Antigone appealed (450-60). Here the chorus is re-
    ferring to the bond of loyalty that Haimon owes Kreon, as son to father. Eros
    evidently "sits beside" such laws "in rule" because he represents an equally
    powerful or even more powerful force. But many commentators have thought
    the text is corrupt here, since Eros often causes the violation of moral laws (cf.
    791-2).

5   I.e. like Haimon, the chorus is carried away by an emotion which outweighs
    their loyalty to Kreon. The metaphor is from chariot racing, where the horses
    might get out of control and carry the driver outside the limits of the course
    (for the image cf. 139, 791-2, 1273-5).

6   On the theme of "marriage to death" see Essay p. 94-5.

ANTIGONE[1]

Look upon me, oh you citizens	*Strophe A*
of this my fatherland,	
as I travel my last road,	
gaze my last on the light of the sun,	
and never again.	810
Hades who puts all to sleep	
leads me still alive	
to the shores of Akheron.[2]	
No wedding hymn is my lot;	
no marriage song sung for me;	815
no, I shall be Akheron's bride.	

CHORUS

But are you not going with praise and renown
to the place where corpses lie concealed?
You were not struck by a wasting sickness
or given the wage that is paid by the sword;[3]   820
you alone among mortals will go down
to Hades still living, a law to yourself.[4]

ANTIGONE

I have heard that Tantalos' daughter,	*Antistrophe A*
our guest who came from Phrygia,	
perished most lamentably	825
upon the peak of Sipylos;[5]	
like tenacious ivy the growth of rock	
tamed her; as she wastes away	

---

1 Antigone sings a monody, or lyric solo, consisting of two strophic pairs and punctuated by groups of lines from the chorus. This may also be viewed as a continuation of the third *stasimon*, in which case the entire lyric contains a total of three strophic pairs, one choral and two monodic.

2 Akheron is one of the rivers of the underworld (the name means "lamentation"). It is personified in 816 as an embodiment of death.

3 A violent death is the "wage" for taking up the sword.

4 Unlike some mythological characters (such as Orpheus and Herakles), Antigone will not actually reach Hades while still living. The chorus simply mean that she is going alive to her tomb. They are trying to comfort her by pointing out that this is an extraordinary fate (if not, as they suggest, a unique one).

5 Antigone counters the chorus' claim that her death is unique by pointing to the parallel with Niobe, whose end resembled her own entombment in the rock. Niobe, daughter of Tantalos, married Amphion, a king of Thebes (thus making her "our guest" to the Theban Antigone). When Niobe boasted that she had many children, whereas Leto, the mother of Apollo and Artemis, had only two, Apollo and Artemis killed all her children. Niobe returned to her original home at Mt. Sipylos (in Ionia), where she was turned into stone, in a rock-formation that some think is still visible today.

the pouring rains never leave her—
so men report—nor does the snow,   830
and under her tearful brow
her shoulder is wet with streams;[1]
most like her a divinity puts me to sleep.

CHORUS

But she was a goddess and born from a god,   —noble, console
while we are mortals and human-born.[2]   835
And yet it is great if people should say
when you perish that you have shared in the lot
of the godlike in life and again in death.[3]

ANTIGONE

Alas, you laugh at me![4]   *Strophe B*
By my fathers' gods, why don't you save   840
this outrage until I have gone?
Why mock me in my presence?
Oh city! Oh city's wealthy men!
Oh springs of Dirce, sacred ground
of Thebes of the fine chariots,   845
you at least I call to witness
how I'm going, unwept by friends,
by what laws I go to the heaped-up prison
of my strange tomb.[5] Unhappy me!
I have no home among mortals,   850

---

1 The chorus describe the misery of Niobe among the storms of the mountain-top, but the language shades into a description of her own unceasing tears for her dead children, which run down her petrified form as mountain streams. In Greek as in English the words "brow" and "shoulder" ("neck" in the Greek) can be applied to mountains as well as people.

2 The chorus counter Antigone's parallel by pointing out what they view as an important difference between the two cases: Niobe was of divine ancestry (she was not, as they claim, a goddess, but her father, Tantalos, was the son of Zeus). The parallel thus enhances Antigone's glory, rather than diminishing it.

3 Antigone resembles Niobe in life as well as in death because she too is meeting death prematurely, and will be covered by a rocky mountain. Her final moment of life, a gruesome confusion of life and death, resembles the moment at which Niobe began to turn to stone.

4 Antigone interprets the chorus's words as mockery, presumably because she was seeking pity from them, but they have instead attempted to console her. On mocking laughter see note on line 551 and Essay p. 79.

5 Antigone's language suggests the piling-up of earth for a grave such as Polyneices' more than a tomb carved into the rock. But the cave-tomb might have an artificially built-up mound on top. It will also be sealed with a pile of stones heaped up at the entrance (cf. 1216).

Commentary about "paying the price" of incest (handwritten marginal note)

no home as a corpse among corpses,
with the living or with the dead.[1]

CHORUS

Stepping forward to daring's very brink,
you stumbled with your foot, my child,
on the lofty pedestal of Justice.[2]   855
You're paying for some ordeal of your father's.

ANTIGONE

You touch on the most distressing   *Antistrophe B*
of all my cares, the thrice-turned
lamentation for my father,[3]
and for that whole destiny   860
allotted to us, the renowned
descendants of Labdacus.
Oh doom of a mother's bed,
ill-fated mother who slept
with her own son, my father!   865
Such was my unhappy birth.
To them I go thus cursed, unmarried,
to dwell without a home.
Oh my brother, the marriage you found
was ill-destined;[4] dying   870
you slaughtered me, who still lived.

CHORUS

There's reverence in revering him;[5]
but power—to those whom power concerns—
cannot permit transgression;

---

1 Antigone laments that, as a living person assigned to the tomb, she belongs properly with neither the living nor the dead. She uses the word *metoikos* (translated "I have no home"), which in fifth-century Athens denotes a resident alien, i.e. a non-Athenian who lives in Athens without civic rights. It also appears at 868 and 890.

2 There is controversy as to whether these lines express approval or disapproval for Antigone's actions. Depending on the exact text adopted, they could mean that Antigone has "tripped over" justice, i.e. violated the justice of Kreon's decree, or "fallen at the feet of justice" as a suppliant, i.e. relied upon the justice of the unwritten laws. The chorus' words at 856 suggest a third interpretation: she has "stumbled against" a larger kind of justice than Kreon's, which requires her to "pay for" the misdeeds of her father Oedipus.

3 I.e. often repeated. The metaphor is from plowing.

4 This refers to Polyneices' marriage to Argeia, daughter of Adrastos, king of Argos, which brought Polyneices the allies he needed to mount his assault on Thebes, and thus indirectly caused Antigone's own death.

5 The chorus acknowledge that Antigone's action was indeed one of reverence, but refuse to dismiss the importance of other conflicting kinds of reverence (such as reverence for a king).

you're destroyed by your self-willed temper.   875
ANTIGONE[1]
Unwept, unfriended, unaccompanied   *Epode*
by wedding song, I'm led away unhappily
along this road prepared for me.
No longer is it lawful for me,
wretch that I am, to look upon   880
the bright eye of this sacred torch;[2]
no friend laments my unwept destiny.[3]
KREON
Do you not know that no one would cease pouring forth
Songs of lament before their death, if that could help?
Lead her away as quickly as you can, and let   885
a covered tomb embrace her, as I said; then leave
her there alone, deserted, whether she desires
to die or live entombed beneath that kind of roof;
for we are pure as far as this girl is concerned;[4]   *b/c they're*
but she shall be deprived of any home up here.   *killing her*   890
ANTIGONE
Oh grave! Oh marriage chamber! Oh you caverned dwelling-
place, eternal prison where I go to join
my own, who perished in such numbers and have been
received by Persephassa with the dead below.[5]
Now I am going down, the last of them, my death   895
the worst by far, before my life has reached its term.
Yet I still nurse the hope that when I get there I
shall come dear to my father, dearly loved by you
my mother, and to you, my own dear brother, dear.[6]
For when you died, with my own hands I washed you and   900
laid out your bodies in due order, gave libations

1 An epode is an additional section of lyric verse sometimes found at the end of a choral song or monody in strophic form. It differs in meter from the preceding strophic pairs.

2 I.e. the sun. The dying often lament that they must leave the sunlight, which stands for life (cf. 809-10).

3 Antigone is not aware of Haimon's distress, and chooses to ignore Ismene's existence (cf. 895). In any case, these two are not present. The chorus have been moved to tears by Antigone's plight (801-5), but Antigone evidently does not count them as "friends."

4 The method of execution is designed to avoid the pollution incurred by killing a blood-relative (cf. 775-6, with note).

5 Persephassa is another name for Persephone, wife of Hades and queen of the dead.

6 I.e. Eteokles, as the change of subject in 902 makes clear.

to your graves. And now it is for tending your
corpse, Polyneices, that I'm reaping this reward.
    Yet, to those with sense I did well to honor you
for I would never have defied the citizens   905
to do this labor if the oozing corpse were that
of my own child, or if my husband lay there dead.
In satisfaction of what law do I say this?[1]
My husband dead, I could have had another, and
a child from someone else, if I had lost the first;   910
but with my mother and my father both concealed
in Hades, no more brothers ever could be born.
By such a law as this I honored you, my own
dear brother, higher than them all; but Kreon thought
that I was doing wrong and daring awful deeds.   915
And now he has me in his hands; he leads me off
unbedded, unaccompanied by wedding song,
without a share in marriage or the nurturing
of children;[2] thus deserted by my friends I go
alive, ill-fated, to the caverns of the dead.   920
What justice of divinities have I transgressed?
Why should I still, unhappy one, look to the gods?
What ally should I call on, when my reverent deed
has gained me condemnation for irreverence?
If this is viewed among the gods as something fine,   925
I'll find out, after suffering, that I was wrong;
but if these men are wrong, may what they suffer be
as evil as the unjust things they do to me.

CHORUS
Still the self-same blasts of the self-same winds
of the spirit are gripping this woman.   930

KREON
Therefore these men who are leading her off
will weep on account of their slowness.

ANTIGONE
Alas! That word has approached very close
to death!

---

1 The curious argument, principle, or "law" that follows has a close parallel in
   Herodotus III.119. (There are also parallels in other cultural traditions.) Many have
   found the argument distasteful or inconsistent with other aspects of Antigone's
   character, and have wished to reject some or all of 904-20 as an interpolation. But
   there are no solid grounds for this excision. See further Essay p. 95-6.

2 The analogy between marriage and death is enhanced by the verb "lead" (916,
   931, 939), also used for a husband "leading" a wife to his house at their wedding (cf. Essay p. 94-5).

KREON

    I do not encourage her to take heart   935
    in hope that this sentence won't be fulfilled.

ANTIGONE

    Oh, my paternal town in the land of Thebes!
    Oh, my ancestral gods!
    Now I'm led off, there is no more delay.
    Look on me, oh rulers of Thebes,[1]   940
    the last of your royal house who remains,[2]
    see what I suffer, from what kind of men,
    for revering reverence.

[Antigone is led away by the guards along the side-entrance leading to the plain.]

CHORUS[3]

    Danae too endured to exchange   *Strophe A*
    heaven's light for a bronze-bound dwelling.[4] 945
    Concealed in a tomb-like bridal chamber,
    she too was yoked.[5]
    Yet she was of honored family, child,
    oh my child, and stored up the seed
    of Zeus in a flow of gold.   950
    Fate is awesome in its power.
    Wealth cannot escape it,
    nor Ares, nor towering walls,
    nor black ships beaten by the salt sea.[6]

---

1 She is addressing the chorus, with the implication that their noble status gives them some authority and / or responsibility for events.

2 Having cut off Ismene for disloyalty, Antigone apparently excludes her from membership of the royal house.

3 The chorus now sing the fourth *stasimon*, which consists of two strophic pairs. Like many choral songs in tragedy, this ode uses mythic parallels to explore the tragic situation. The text of the song is exceptionally corrupt and obscure, but the various stories all involve a person of noble birth being imprisoned, like Antigone. (See Essay p. 97).

4 Danae's father, Acrisios, was warned by an oracle that he would be killed by his daughter's son. So he shut up Danae to keep her from becoming pregnant. But Zeus impregnated her in the form of a golden shower, and she gave birth to the hero Perseus.

5 I.e. she had to submit to her fate (cf. 956). But the metaphor also suggests the "yoking" of a woman in marriage (cf. Essay p. 85).

6 I.e. fate cannot be bribed with wealth, fought off with warfare, kept out by walls, or escaped by sea-faring.

And the son of Dryas, quick to rage, was yoked,   *Antistrophe A*
king of the Edonians, imprisoned by Dionysos   956
in rocky bondage for his raging taunts.[1]
Thus did the awful blossoming force
of his madness dwindle, drop by drop.
He did not recognize the god   960
until he attacked him in madness
with taunting tongue. He tried to stop
the women possessed by the god,
their fires and their cries of *Euoi!*
and provoked the flute-loving Muses.[2]   965

By the waters of the Dark Rocks,   *Strophe B*
and of the double sea,
are the shores of Bosporus,
and Thracian Salmydessus,[3]
where neighboring Ares looked upon   970
the accursed blinding wound
dealt to Phineus's two sons
by his savage wife, a wound
that darkened the orbs of their eyes,
calling for vengeance, gouged out   975
by bloody hands and a sharp shuttle.[4]

Wasting away, that wretched pair,   *Antistrophe B*
they wept for their wretched fate,
offspring born of a mother
whose marriage was no marriage.   980
Her own seed made her queen
of the ancient-born Erekhthids;[5]

---

1 Lykourgos, son of Dryas, resisted the arrival of the god Dionysos in Thrace (north of Greece), so Dionysos drove him mad. He did many violent deeds and was finally imprisoned in a cave.

2 The "women possessed by the god" are the Bacchants or Maenads, the female worshipers of Dionysos (cf. n. 34). *Euoi!* is their ritual cry (cf. 1134-6). The Muses (goddesses of music, poetry, song and dance) are also sometimes found in the company of Dionysos.

3 Salmydessus is in Thrace, on the west coast of the Black Sea, near the entrance to the Bosporus. Thrace was the home of Ares, god of war.

4 Kleopatra was the daughter of the wind-god Boreas and wife of Phineus, King of Salmydessus. She bore her husband two sons, but he imprisoned her and married another wife, named Eidothea. Eidothea blinded Kleopatra's sons with a shuttle (a long, pointed, needle-like implement used in weaving), and had them imprisoned too. (Note that this Kleopatra has nothing to do with the famous Egyptian queen.)

5 Kleopatra's mother was Oreithyia, daughter of Erekhtheus, a mythical king of Athens. His descendants are called the Erekhthids.

she was nurtured in far-off caves,
among her father's storm-winds,
a horse-swift Boread over the steep hills,   985
a child of gods.[1] Yet on her too
the long-lived Fates bore down, my child.

[Enter Teiresias, a blind old prophet, by the side-entrance coming from Thebes proper; he is guided by a young boy.]

TEIRESIAS
Oh lords of Thebes, we've come here by a road we shared,
two seeing through the eyes of one; for this is how
a blind man makes his way, with someone else to lead.   990

KREON
What is it, aged Teiresias? Do you have news?

TEIRESIAS
I'll tell you. You, believe the prophet and obey.

KREON
I've not departed from your thinking in the past.[2]

TEIRESIAS
And that is why you've steered this city's course aright.

KREON
I can attest the benefits that I've received.   995

TEIRESIAS
Think now you stand again on fortune's razor-edge.

KREON
What is it? How I shudder at the words you speak!

TEIRESIAS
You'll find out when you hear the signs from my skilled craft.
As I sat on the ancient seat where I perform
my augury, a haven for all kinds of birds,[3]   1000
I heard the birds give unknown voice, screeching
in evil frenzy, babbling incoherently.
I sensed them tearing at each other with their bloody

---

1 Boreas the wind-god carried Oreithyia off to a distant mountainous region of Thrace, where she bore him four children, one of whom was Kleopatra. His daughters are called Boreads.

2 This may allude to the fate of Kreon's son Megareus (sometimes called Menoikeus), who was sacrificed, on the advice of Teiresias, to save the city from its attackers (cf. 1301-5).

3 Augury was an important kind of divination, in which omens were taken from the flight patterns and behavior of birds. They were lured with food to a "haven" so that they could be more easily observed.

claws—the whirring of their wings was a clear sign.
At once, in fear, I tried to make burnt-sacrifice   1005
upon an altar duly kindled; but Hephaistos
did not blaze forth from the offerings;[1] instead
a putrid liquid from the thighs oozed out upon
the coals, and smoked and spattered, and the gall-bladder
exploded up into the air; the thighs, streaming   1010
with moisture, lay bared of their covering of lard.
I learned about these things—the failure of my rites
of prophecy, which gave no signs—from this boy here.
For just as I lead others onward, he leads me.
        And it's from *your* bad thinking that the city is   1015
so sick. Our public altars and our hearths have all
been tainted, every one, by dogs and birds with food
from the ill-fated fallen son of Oedipus.
And this is why the gods accept our sacrificial
prayers no more, nor flames from burning victims' thighs,   1020
nor do the birds scream cries that give me signs,
for they have eaten of a slain man's bloody fat.
        Think on this well, my child. To go wrong is a thing
shared by all humans. But when someone does go wrong,
that man's no longer foolish or unfortunate   1025
if he attempts to heal the evil he has fallen
into, and does not remain immovable.
Self-will is what incurs the charge of foolishness.
Yield to the dead and don't keep stabbing at a perished
man. What prowess is it to re-kill the dead?   1030
I think and speak for your own good; it is most sweet
to learn from one who speaks well, if it profits you.

KREON

 Old man, you all keep shooting arrows at me, just
like archers at a target.[2] Even your prophetic
skill is used against me. For a long time now   1035
I have been traded by your breed like merchandise.[3]
Go, make your profits! Keep on trading silver-gold

---

1 When augury fails, Teiresias turns to another method of divination, burnt-
   sacrifice, where omens were provided by the manner in which the offering
   burned. The offering itself consisted of an animal's thigh-bones, wrapped with
   a double layer of fat, with intestines and gall-bladder on top. The use of
   Hephaistos' name for "fire" here suggests divine disapproval (cf. n. on 124).

2 "You all" must refer to the other imagined conspirators, and perhaps Haimon.

3 I.e. Teiresias has allegedly taken bribes to plot against Kreon, and thus "sold"
   him as a piece of merchandise. Kreon may be referring to the death of Menoikeus
   (see n. on 993).

from Sardis,[1] if you wish, and gold from India;
but you shall not conceal him in a tomb, not even
if the eagles, birds of Zeus, should wish to rend   1040
his flesh and take it up to Zeus's throne as food.[2]
Not even then will I let him be buried out
of fear of this pollution. I know well no human
has the strength to bring pollution to the gods.[3]
But mortals, even those with many awesome skills,   *old*   1045
                                                    senile
fall shamefully, oh aged Teiresias, when they
speak finely shameful words for profit's sake.

TEIRESIAS
Ah![4]   ← *shift in favor of speaker*
Does any mortal know, or take into account...

KREON
What thing? What maxim shared by all is this you speak?

TEIRESIAS
...how far good counsel is the best thing to possess?   1050

KREON
As far, I think, as thoughtlessness does greatest harm.

TEIRESIAS
Yet this is just the sickness that is tainting you.   — *Both*
                                                       Haimon &
KREON   *chorus talk*
I'd rather not abuse a prophet in reply.   *about good*
                                                       consoul
TEIRESIAS
You do so, when you say my prophecies are false.

KREON
They are! All prophets are a money-loving breed.   1055

TEIRESIAS
And kings a breed that loves to profit shamefully.

KREON
Do you not know that you are talking to a king?

TEIRESIAS
I know; that through me it's you've kept this city safe.

---

1 This refers to electrum, a natural alloy of silver and gold, also called "white
   gold," which came from mines near Sardis in Lydia.
2 The eagle, king of birds, was sacred to Zeus, king of gods.
3 A human being could not literally taint the gods, but of course this does not
   mean Zeus approves of Kreon's behavior.
4 Such an exclamation interjected into stichomythia (single-line dialogue) often
   indicates a power-shift in favor of the speaker (so also at 323).

KREON

You are a clever prophet, but you love injustice.

TEIRESIAS

You'll make me tell things still unmoved within my mind.   1060

KREON

Let them be moved! Just do not speak for profit's sake.

TEIRESIAS

Is that what I'm already doing, in your view?

KREON

Know that you'll never use my thinking for your trade![1]

TEIRESIAS

And you, know well you shall not live through many more
swift-racing courses of the sun before you give   1065
a child of your own flesh and blood in turn, a corpse
to pay for corpses, since you've cast below a person
who belongs above, making a living soul
reside within a tomb dishonorably, and keep
up here a corpse belonging to the gods below,   1070
deprived of rites, of offerings, of piety.
You have no business with such things; nor do the upper
gods, but in this you're committing violence.
Therefore the ruinous late-avenging Furies of
the gods and Hades lie in wait for you, that you   1075
may be caught up in these same evils in your turn.
See if I'm saying this because I'm silver-plated![2]
A little time will test my metal, showing forth
both men's and women's wailing cries in your own house.[3]
Moreover all those cities have been shaken up   1080
with enmity whose mangled flesh got funeral rites
from dogs, or beasts, or flying birds that carried home

---

1 I.e. Teiresias will not be able to make money out of the alleged Theban conspirators by getting Kreon to change his mind.

2 Teiresias refers sardonically to Kreon's repeated claims that he has been bribed,
or "covered in silver." The test of time, like a touchstone, will reveal that the
prophet is not "plated" with any superficial appearances, but is authentic
through and through.

3 The phrase is ambiguous between "wailing *by* men and women" and "wailing
for men and women," and both will turn out to be true. The prophesied wails
of mourning will be heard before the play ends (1207, 1227, 1303, 1316). They
are the direct result of Kreon's prohibition on such wailing for Polyneices (28,
204; cf. also 423).

the impious stench to every city and its hearths.[1]
    In rage have I let fly these arrows, archer-like,
against your heart, since you have pained me; they are sure,   1085
and running will not help you to escape their fire.
    Come, child, lead me away to my own house, so that
this man can let his rage fly forth at younger men,
and learn to nurse a tongue that is more peaceable,
a mind that's better than the thoughts he's thinking now.   1090

[Exit Teiresias, led by his attendant, down the side-entrance into the city.]

CHORUS
My lord, the man has gone from us with awful words
of prophecy. And since the black hair on my head
first turned to white, I know that he has never uttered
to the city anything that turned out false.

KREON
I know it too, and I am shaken in my mind.   1095
To yield is awful; but, by standing firm, to strike
with ruin my proud heart—why, that is awful too.

CHORUS
You need to take good counsel now, Menoikeus' son.

KREON
What should I do then? Tell me, and I shall obey.

CHORUS
Go, set the girl free from her rocky chamber, and   1100
construct a tomb for him who's lying there exposed.

KREON
Is this what you advise? You think that I should yield?

CHORUS
As quickly as you can, my lord. The gods' avenging
Harms, swift-footed, cut down those with evil thoughts.[2]

KREON
Alas! Reluctantly I leave my heart's resolve: 1105
I'll do it. There's no fighting with necessity.

CHORUS
Go, then, and do it. Don't assign this task to others.

---

1 This refers to the cities allied with Polyneices in his campaign against Thebes. Kreon has refused burial not just to Polyneices, but to all the dead of the attacking army (a central feature of the story in many other treatments). Their only "entombment" has been within the stomachs of wild animals. This causes both pollution (transmitted by birds of prey) and resentment in the dead men's home cities.

2 The Harms of the gods are personified forces of vengeance like the Furies (1074-5).

KREON

> I'll go at once. Go! Go, all my attendants, both
> those present and those absent![1] Take up axes in
> your hands, and rush towards the place—it's over there.   1110
> And now that my opinion has reversed itself,
> I shall be there to set her free, just as I was
> the one who bound her. It is best, I fear, to live
> until life's end preserving the established laws.

[Exit Kreon with attendants, along the side-entrance leading to the plain.]

CHORUS[2]

> Oh you of many names,   *Strophe A*
> treasure of the Kadmean bride,   1116
> child of deep-thundering Zeus,[3]
> who care for famous Italy,[4]
> and hold sway in Demeter's
> folding hollows at Eleusis,   1120
> a sanctuary shared by all,[5]
> oh Bacchus, dwelling in Thebes,
> the Bacchants' mother-city,
> by Ismenos' flowing stream,
> at the sowing of the savage dragon's seed![6]   1125
> The smoky flash of the torch   *Antistrophe A*
> has seen you,
> above the double-peaked rock,
> where the Korycian Nymphs,
> the Bacchants tread,   1130

---

1 Apparently an idiomatic expression meaning "every one of you."

2 The fifth and last *stasimon* is a hymn to Dionysos, the chief god of Thebes, in two strophic pairs. As often in Sophocles, the chorus is hopeful and sings joyfully just before the final calamity.

3 Dionysos was the son of Zeus and Semele, daughter of Kadmos (founder of Thebes). Semele asked Zeus to appear to her in the form in which he showed himself to his divine wife Hera. He came with his thunder and lightning, and she was incinerated.

4 There were many Greek colonies in southern Italy, and Dionysos often appears in art of that region.

5 Demeter is goddess of earth and fertility. Her most prominent cult was at Eleusis, near Athens. "Hollows" alludes to the topography of Eleusis, but also to the receptive bosom or womb of the earth mother. Dionysos was also worshiped here under the name Iakkhos (cf. 1154). The Eleusinian cult was open to all, and many flocked to the festivals; hence it is "shared by all."

6 Kadmos founded Thebes by sowing dragon's teeth, from which the first Thebans grew (cf. 126 with note). It is the "mother-city" of the Bacchants because the god was born there. Ismenos was a river to the east of the city.

and so has the stream of Kastalia .[1]
The ivy-covered slopes
of Nysa's mountains have sent you,
and the green shore clustered with grapes.[2]
Immortal songs cry out *Euoi!* to you   1135
watching over the streets of Thebes.

You honor this city most highly,   *Strophe B*
high above all the rest,
you along with your mother,
she who was struck by lightning.   1140
Since all of the city's people
are gripped by a violent sickness,
come now too with purifying foot,
over the ridge of Parnassus,
or the groaning waters of the strait.[3]   1145

Oh you who lead the chorus   *Antistrophe B*
of stars that breath forth fire,[4]
you who watch over the voices
that cry out during the night,
offspring born of Zeus,   1150
appear to us, oh lord,
with your attendant Thyiads,[5]
who dance all night in madness
for bountiful Iakkhos!

[Enter Messenger, along the side-entrance leading to the plain. He is an atten-
dant of Kreon, probably a slave.[6]]

1 The Bacchants celebrated Dionysos with torches and dancing at night in the
   mountains. At Delphi they danced on the high ground of Mt. Parnassus above
   two rocky peaks but below the mountain's summit. The Kastalian stream flows
   down from here to Delphi. Here the Bacchants are not human women, but
   local nymphs, named for the Korycian cave, a large cave on Mt. Parnassus a
   few miles from Delphi.
2 These mountains and vineyards are at Nysa in Euboea, an island north of Attica
   which was famous for its wine (see Map of Attica). Dionysos had an important
   cult here. Ivy and grapes were both sacred to this god, who is associated with
   lush fertility.
3 I.e. the strait between Euboea and the mainland.
4 The heavenly bodies were thought to participate in the night-time rituals of
   Iakkhos (Dionysos) at Eleusis.
5 Another name for the nymphs who accompany Dionysos.
6 The Messenger is a standard formal device in Greek tragedy. He is a barely
   characterized minor figure whose function is to report off-stage events, often
   of a violent or shocking nature.

MESSENGER

Neighbors of Kadmos and the house of Amphion,[1]   1155
there is no human life in any state that I
would ever praise or criticize as something fixed.
For fortune sets upright and fortune dashes down
whoever has good luck or bad at any time.
No prophet can tell mortals the established truth.   1160
Kreon was once a man to envy, in my view.
He saved this land of Kadmos from its enemies,
gained total power in the land and guided it,
sowed children's noble seed and throve in them.
Now all is gone. When even a man's pleasures let   1165
him down, then I no longer count him as alive—
I just consider him to be a living corpse.
Heap wealth within your house, if you so wish, and live
with royal show; and yet if joy is missing from
all this, I would not pay smoke's shadow to buy all   1170
the rest from any man, compared to pleasure.

CHORUS

What further weight of grief do you bring for our kings?

MESSENGER

They're dead. The living are responsible for death.

CHORUS

Who is the bloody murderer? Who lies dead? Speak!

MESSENGER

Haimon has perished, bloodied by one close to home.[2]   1175

CHORUS

Was it his father's hand that did it, or his own?

MESSENGER

He killed himself, in wrath at blood his father shed.

CHORUS

How right, oh prophet, did you prove your words to be!

MESSENGER

That's how things stand; you may take counsel for the rest.

[Enter Eurydike from the palace, attended by maids.[3]]

---

1 Amphion was a king of Thebes who built the city walls by charming the stones
   into place with the music of his lyre.

2 The Greek word could mean "by his own hand" or "by the hand of a kinsman."
   Hence the chorus' need for further clarification. The pun on Haimon's name
   and the Greek word for blood (*haima*) is particularly striking here (cf. n. on 794).

3 This character may have been invented by Sophocles. She has nothing to do
   with Orpheus' wife of the same name.

CHORUS

But here is Kreon's wife, wretched Eurydike,   1180
close by; I see her coming from the house. She must
have heard about her son, or else she's here by chance.

EURYDIKE

Assembled townsfolk, I was starting to go out
and overheard you. I was going to supplicate
the goddess Pallas,[1] to address her with my prayers.   1185
As I was loosening the bolts across the door
to open it, a voice assailed my ears with words
of evil to our house. I sank back, full of dread,
upon my serving-maids, quite stricken from my wits.
But speak again, whatever news you brought, and I   1190
shall listen—I'm experienced in suffering.[2]

MESSENGER

Dear mistress, I was there in person and I'll speak
without omitting even one word of the truth.
Why should I try to soothe you with soft words that will
be shown as falsehoods later? Truth is always right.   1195
        I went, attending on your husband as his guide,
up to the high part of the plain where Polyneices'
corpse still lay unpitied, mangled by the dogs.
We prayed first to the goddess of the road and Pluto
to restrain their rage and to be kind,[3] and washed   1200
him with the ritual washing, then with branches freshly
plucked we burned the body—what was left of it—
and built a lofty grave-mound from the earth that was
his home,[4] then made our way towards the prison of
the girl, her bridal-cave of Hades, strewn with rock.[5]   1205
Near that unhallowed inner chamber someone heard
a distant sound of high-pitched wailing cries, and came
to tell our master Kreon of these signs. As he
drew closer, miserable cries which gave no signs

1 Pallas is a frequent name for Athena, the patron goddess of Athens.

2 This presumably alludes to the death of her son Megareus (see n. on 993).

3 The "goddess of the road" is Hekate, an underworld goddess to whom offerings were left at the junctions of roads. She is sometimes identified with Persephone, queen of the underworld. Pluto is another name for Hades, king of the underworld.

4 After a corpse was burned, the bones were collected and a mound of earth piled over them. Polyneices is buried in his native ("home") soil, but the Greek also suggests that under the earth is where he, as a dead person, belongs.

5 Another inverted reference to marriage, since a bridal chamber would normally be strewn with soft bedding, perfumed and decorated with flowers.

surrounded him; he moaned aloud and sent forth words   1210
of bitter lamentation, "Ah, wretch that I am,
am I a prophet? Am I moving down a path
that's more unfortunate than any road I've walked
before? My son's voice greets me. Servants, come,
go closer quickly! Go up to the tomb and enter   1215
by that gap where stones have been torn out, up to
the grave's own mouth, and look to see if I detect
the voice of Haimon, or the gods deceive my ears."
At this command from our downhearted master we
looked in; within the furthest recess of the tomb   1220
we saw the maiden hanging by her neck, tied up
there by a noose of finely woven cloth;[1] the boy
had flung himself around her waist in close embrace,
while he bemoaned his bridal-bed now lost below,
his father's deeds and his unhappy marriage-bed.   1225
When Kreon saw them, he moaned horribly and went
inside to him, and called out with a wailing cry:
"What deed is this you've done, bold wretch! What came into
your mind? By what disaster did you lose your wits?
Come out, my child, I beg you as a suppliant!"[2]   1230
His son glared back at him with savage eyes, spat in
his face, said nothing in reply, and drew his two-
edged sword. His father rushed back to escape and Haimon
missed his aim. At once, ill-fated boy, in anger
at himself, he tensed himself upon his sword-   1235
point and drove half the blade into his side. Before
his wits departed he embraced the maiden with
a wilting arm; gasping, he spurted forth a sharp
swift stream of bloody drops upon the girl's white cheek.
He lies there, corpse embracing corpse. He has received   1240
his marriage rites at last—poor wretch—in Hades' house,
and demonstrated to the human race how far
ill-counsel is the greatest evil for a man.

[Exit Eurydike with her maids into the palace.]

CHORUS

What do you think this means? The woman's gone again
without one word of good or evil from her lips.   1245

---

1 Antigone has hanged herself with a piece of her own clothing, probably her
   veil (see Essay p. 101).

2 Kreon invokes the ritual of supplication, which imposes moral and religious
   obligation on the addressee, but also places the speaker in a socially subordinate or even humiliating position (cf. Essay p. 102-3).

MESSENGER
I am astonished too. But I'm sustained by hope
that hearing of this grief for her own child she won't
think fit to make lament before the city, but
will set her maids to mourn this household woe inside.[1]
She's too experienced in judgment to do wrong.   1250

CHORUS
I don't know; but I think that silence in excess
is just as weighty as extraordinary cries.

MESSENGER
I'll go inside the house, then I shall know if she
is really keeping something secretly concealed,
pent up within her raging heart. Your words are good: 1255
excessive silence also carries heavy weight.

*[Exit Messenger into the palace. Enter Kreon along the side-entrance leading
from the plain, carrying Haimon's corpse.[2]]*

CHORUS
But here is our lord himself; he comes
with a clear-stamped monument held in his hands.
If it's lawful to say so,[3] his doom wasn't caused
by any outsider—he did wrong himself.   1260

KREON
        Oh!   *Strophe A*
The rigid wrongs, death-dealing,
of thoughtless wrongful thinking!
Oh you who here behold us,
kinsmen who killed and died!

---

1   This does not mean that Eurydike herself should not lament, but that she should
    do so unostentatiously, in antiphonal lamentation with her maids inside the
    house.

2   Alternatively, Haimon's body may be carried in by attendants, while he em-
    braces it with gestures of mourning. (This would provide a closer dramatic
    echo of Antigone's final scene.) In either case, there is a contrast between what
    Kreon holds "in his hands" now and previously (cf. 916, 1258, 1280, 1297, 1344).
    No further mention is made, here or elsewhere, of Antigone's body.

    There follows a *kommos*, or lyric dialogue of lamentation, between the Chorus
    and Kreon (1261-1347). It is preceded and followed by choral anapests (1257-
    60, 1348-53). Kreon's lyric lamentations alternate with spoken lines (iambic
    trimeters) from Kreon, the chorus leader, and the second messenger, in a com-
    plex symmetrical structure.

3   The chorus is hesitant because of Kreon's royal status and the enormity of the
    charge they are making. The word they use for "lawful" is *themis*, which refers not
    to human laws but to a sense of what is divinely permitted in the order of things.
    A related word is used for the "mighty ordinances" in the ode to Eros (798).

Alas for my counsels' misfortune!   1265
Oh my son, too young
for your youthful doom!
Aiai! Aiai! You died, you departed,
through my ill counsel, not your own!

CHORUS

Alas! You seem now to see justice, but too late.   1270

KREON

Alas!
I have learned, wretch that I am! On my head
a god with a mighty weight struck down
at that moment, and tossed me in savage roads,
overthrew my joy—*alas!*—to be trampled.[1]   1275
Ah! Ah! Oh alas for the labors,
the toilsome labors of mortals!

[*Enter Messenger, from the palace.*]

MESSENGER

You seem, my master, to have come with evils, yet
you have more still in store; the first you bear in your
own hands, but soon you will see others in the house.   1280

KREON

What greater evil follows evils such as these?

MESSENGER

Your wife is dead—in truth the mother of this corpse[2] —
unhappy woman, killed just now by fresh-struck blows.

KREON

Oh!   *Antistrophe A*
Oh harbor of Hades, unpurifiable,[3]
why, oh why are you destroying me?   1285
Oh herald of sorrow's evil tidings,
what word is this you utter?
Aiai! You've re-killed a man destroyed!
What are you telling me, boy?[4]

---

1 The wording here suggests the image of a charioteer who drives recklessly
   into disaster after a blow on the head.

2 She is Haimon's mother "in truth" because his death drives her to suicide,
   thus showing that she is a complete mother, one who cares exclusively about
   her children.

3 Hades is here viewed as a harbor choked with an endless supply of putrid
   corpses, and hence of pollution.

4 This is addressed to the messenger. Slaves were commonly addressed this way,
   or it could be merely the address of an older man to a youth.

What new slaughter do you say
embraces me—*Aiai! Aiai!* —   1290
on top of destruction a woman's doom?[1]

[The palace doors open to reveal the corpse of Eurydike.[2]]

CHORUS
She can be seen. She is no longer shut indoors.

[handwritten marginal note: I see he put Antigone in palace]

KREON
Alas!
Ah wretched me! I see this second evil!   1295
What destiny, what still awaits me?
I've just held my child in my hands,
wretch that I am, and now I see her,
another corpse before me.
Ah, ah, miserable mother! Ah my child!   1300

MESSENGER
There at the altar with a sharply-whetted knife[3]
she let her eyes close into darkness, after she
wailed first for dead Megareus' empty bed and then
for Haimon's.[4] Last she sang out evil curses on
your head, because you were the killer of your sons.[5]   1305

KREON
Aiai! Aiai!   *Strophe B*
My heart leaps with fear! Why does no one
strike my chest with a two-edged sword?
Wretched am I—*aiai!*—   1310
dissolved in wretched anguish!

---

1 Kreon means that he is overcome by his wife's death, yet the phrase also hints
   at his own now emasculated condition (see Essay p. 103).

2 The *ekkuklēma*—a low wheeled platform (above, p. 9-10)—may have been used
   here, showing Eurydike lying at the altar where she stabbed herself. Alternatively, attendants may bring out her body and place it beside Kreon, who is
   thus framed by the two corpses. The latter would make good dramatic sense
   of 1340-42.

3 This line is conjectural, since the Greek is corrupt.

4 On Megareus see n. on 993. The phrase "empty bed" is an emendation, and its
   meaning is uncertain. It may refer to the fact that neither of Eurydike's sons
   reached maturity as marked by marriage, which would fit in well with the
   play's theme of thwarted marriage. Alternatively, it could mean she lamented
   her own bed bereft first of Megareus and then Haimon. On this interpretation,
   she is lamenting the loss of her young, like the mother-bird to which Antigone
   is compared at 424-5. This also resonates strongly with the play's themes of
   incest and thwarted motherhood.

5 It was believed that the curse of a suicide was especially powerful in bringing
   revenge.

MESSENGER
  Before she died, your wife denounced you as the one
  responsible for both the dooms of your two sons.

KREON
  By just what form of bloody slaughter did she go?

MESSENGER
  She struck with her own hand into her liver, when   1315
  she heard of her son's death, so piercingly bewailed.[1]

KREON
  Alas! Alas!
  To me, to no other mortal,
  this responsibility will cling forever.
  It was I who killed you, I, wretch that I am!   1320
  It was I! I speak truly.
  Oh, servants!
  Lead me as quick as you can,
  lead me out of the way,
  I who exist no more than nothing.   1325

CHORUS
  If any profit lies in evils, your advice
  holds profit. Evils in our way are best when briefest.

KREON
  Let it come, let it come!   *Antistrophe B*
  Let that finest of fates for me appear,
  bringing my final day,   1330
  supremely best of fates!
  Let it come, let it come,
  that I may never see another day!

CHORUS
  That's in the future. Now we must perform what lies
  at hand. They care about these matters who should care.[2]   1335

KREON
  My prayer encompassed all my passionate desires.

CHORUS
  Pray now no further. There is no deliverance
  for mortals from whatever is ordained for them.

---

1 Greek texts often speak of the liver, as well as the heart, as a seat of life and an
   organ affected by passionate emotions. But it also refers more loosely to the
   vital organs.

2 This may mean that the gods, in whose hands the future lies, will take care of
   the future, including Kreon's death, or that the chorus themselves, and Kreon,
   will take care of the present situation.

KREON

> Lead me away, a worthless man.
> I killed you, my son, without intending to,   1340
> you too, my wife—ah, wretch that I am!
> I cannot look towards either one.
> Nowhere can I lean for support.
> All in my hands is warped,[1]
> and from outside   1345
> a crushing destiny
> has leapt down on my head.

[Kreon's attendants lead him into the palace.[2]]

CHORUS

> *Sound thought is by far the foremost rule*
> *of happiness; when we deal with the gods*
> *we should never act with irreverence.*   1350
> *Mighty words of boastful men*
> *are paid for with mighty blows which teach*
> *sound thinking at last in old age.*

---

1 There is an ambiguity here between "the situation I am handling" and "what I have in my arms."

2 It is possible that Kreon departs down one of the side-entrances, in a funeral cortège with the bodies of Haimon and Eurydike. But an exit into the house is suggested by 1324, and would provide a fitting symbol of his ultimate emasculation (Essay p. 103).

Antigone: Interpretive Essay

When I moved to Seattle in 1985, I encountered two graffiti written one above the other on the same wall, in two different colors and by two different hands. One of them said, "Born to be arrested!", the other, "OBEY ALL LAWS! BE A MODEL CITIZEN!" These slogans might have been written by Antigone and Kreon respectively. (Antigone's name even means something like "born in opposition," whereas Kreon's means "ruler.") Taken together, they pithily summarize Sophocles' tragedy in the way that it has most often been viewed, that is as a drama of antinomies. As such it explores the multiple tensions between the household and the city-state (Greek *oikos* and *polis*), the individual and society, male and female, divine and human, nature and convention (Greek *phusis* and *nomos*), young and old. But although many of these polarities are enshrined in the two main characters, that does not mean the characters themselves are mere symbols. Rather, ideas are explored in the play as embodied in specific dramatic persons. Sophocles does not present us with a clash of abstractions, such as "the city" vs. "the family," but with vividly realized characters embodying particular sets of values, emotions and circumstances, which in turn are shaped by such factors as gender, age, and social status.

In keeping with the diametrical opposition between Antigone and Kreon, and their utter failure to connect with each other, Sophocles introduces them to us discretely, in separate scenes divided by the Chorus' entry song (*parodos*). The two scenes in question are markedly different in tone and dramatic effect. The prologue shows us two young women alone together in front of the outer gates of the palace courtyard. Antigone addresses her sister in the first line with an untranslatable expression, literally, "shared self-sister head of Ismene," which conveys an intense sense of familial identity and closeness. The time is just before dawn. There is an element of transgression and risk in the fact that two young unmarried girls are outside the palace gates, rather than inside in the space culturally defined as female. As respectable women, Antigone and her sister do not normally venture out (cf. 578-9), but must evidently do so in order to be alone together without being overheard (18-19). The moment is private, female, and conspiratorial in atmosphere.

Antigone's opening speech establishes many of the principal themes of the play, including friendship and enmity, the ill-fated family of Oedipus, and Kreon's recent proclamation. She herself emerges at the outset as fiercely dedicated to the ties of family and "friendship." In ancient Greek culture these are not two distinct concepts. The word translated as "friendship" (*philia*) is much broader than its English equivalent, embracing not just personal friends but anyone with whom one has a relationship of mutual obligation. In this sense, even the lowly Guard may view Antigone as a *philos* or "friend" (438). The emotions that we associate with friendship may be present, and often are, but they are not essential. Chief among such "friends" are one's close family members. And this is the variety of "friendship" to which Antigone is firmly committed (cf. 523). Unlike Ismene, she is not a loving personality in a modern sense, but cold and harsh to those around her. It is her commitment to the "friendship" of blood-kinship that fuels her devotion to Polyneices. This devotion is passionate (cf. 423-8), but there is no sign that it is directed towards Polyneices as a distinct individual. There is no indication, for example, that if Eteokles had been the traitor who attacked Thebes her present behavior would be any different (cf. 900-902). It is blood-kinship per se to which she is committed. Nor does she show any interest in other kinds of "friends," such as those one chooses for oneself. In this she is contrasted with Kreon, who explicitly speaks of friends that one "makes for oneself," and ranks any form of *philia* as secondary to the state (182-90).

These different attitudes towards friendship form part of a larger network of oppositions between the family or household (*oikos*) and the state (*polis*). The household is the female realm in Greek culture, so it is appropriate that a woman would count familial *philia* above other kinds of friendship, and specifically above loyalty to the external, male world of the *polis*. But Kreon's first priority, as a man and a king, is the well-being of the state. For him, therefore, the primary focus of friendship is political alliance, and personal ties of any kind must not be allowed to interfere with the well-being of the *polis* as a whole. This tension between *oikos* and *polis* reflects Athenian historical tensions between the rise of democracy and the traditional influence of powerful aristocratic families. From this perspective, Kreon's preference for the *polis* accords with democratic ideology, though he takes it to a radical extreme. The tension between *oikos* and *polis* is also related to a pervasive fifth-century intellectual debate concerning the relative importance of "nature" (*phusis*) and "convention" (*nomos*). Antigone's conception of *philia* is a "natural" one, based in the ties of blood-kinship. But Kreon treats *philia* as something "conventional," that is, as something made and controlled by human beings. This contrast extends to other aspects of their opposition, especially Antigone's preference for the "unwritten" laws of the gods, viewed as grounded in the natural order of things, over the man-made law of Kreon (below, p. 87). The opposition between *nomos* and *phusis* is also frequently gendered, with the "natural" more closely linked to the female, and the "conventional" to the male.

From the perspective of family loyalty, Kreon's edict is an outrage, since the burial of dead kin was a powerful social and religious obligation.

At the same time, Polyneices is indisputably a traitor, and denial of burial was a punishment sometimes meted out to such traitors, and other extreme criminals, in Sophocles' Athens. The original audience would therefore not automatically have viewed denial of burial with such abhorrence as Antigone does. Yet Kreon's measure is very extreme. First of all, he is himself the head of the family, and as such has a personal obligation to bury both his nephews. Secondly, he denies the body burial under any circumstances whatsoever. In Athens, the family of a dead traitor was permitted to bury the body outside Athenian territory--a compromise juggling the competing demands of state and family, public needs and religion, policy and personal feelings. In other situations, unburied corpses of criminals were thrown into a chasm or into the sea. In no case were they left unburied and exposed near human habitation for a prolonged period of time. The primary emphasis of Sophocles' play is on the foulness and pollution, physical and moral, of leaving any body unburied (29-30, 205-6; cf. below, p. 97-8). This transcends both familial and political forms of obligation, suggesting a larger truth about the relationship of humans to their world as a whole, natural and divine as well as personal and political.

The closeness between the two sisters in the prologue is established only to be ruptured, when Antigone declares her intention to bury their brother and Ismene demurs. Their different attitudes towards this issue place them in very different alignments with the norms of ancient Greek femininity. Mourning and the performance of proper funeral rites for dead family members were important female social and religious functions (cf. 1246-9). Women were responsible for washing and laying out the corpse and ritual wails of mourning, as well as visiting the grave with libations (cf. 900-902), all of which Kreon has explicitly forbidden in the case of Polyneices (27-8, 203-4). Despite the strong association of women with life inside the house, funerals and other religious rituals were the primary occasions on which it was appropriate, and indeed necessary, for women to appear in public (cf. 1183-5). So Antigone's concern with mourning, together with her devotion to the family and the "natural," and her lack of interest in the male world of the *polis*, are culturally "feminine" traits.

On the other hand, the most desirable virtue of women was *sōphrosunē*, an important virtue covering self-control, moderation, awareness of one's proper place, and deference to authority. By showing such deference Ismene presents herself as a "good girl" who acknowledges her own inferiority and weakness (61-8). As a woman who stays properly within the house, she has heard nothing of the latest news from the external, political world of men (16-17), whereas Antigone somehow knows of the public proclamation (447-8). Ismene also embodies other Greek stereotypes about women: she is highly emotional (cf. 526-30), concerned about marriage (568-74), secretive and deceptive (cf. 531-4, 493-5). She urges Antigone to conceal her plan (84-5) and later lies about her own role (536-7). When she uses the "masculine" language of warfare and hunting it is only to emphasize the weakness that she attributes to their feminine "nature" (61-2; cf. 66, 78-9, 92). Against this concept of "natural" "feminine" weakness, Antigone juxtaposes an appeal to "nature" of a different kind: an appeal to the heroic nature that comes from noble birth (38). The question of what is "natural" to women, men, individual people or human beings in general, will be an issue throughout the play (cf. 439, 501, 523, 688, 721).

Paradoxically, Ismene's "appropriate" female deference means that in the absence of male approval she is unwilling to participate in the female activity of mourning. Antigone, on the other hand, asserts herself in a "masculine" way in order to carry out the deed. The need for assertive, "masculine" action is caused by circumstances outside her control, but her character is well fitted to perform it. Her symbolic rejection of the female sphere is indicated from the start, by the fact that she has brought Ismene outside the walls of the house. She then undertakes not only the female functions of washing, mourning, and giving offerings to the corpse, but the actual burial, which was normally carried out by men. In her emotions, values and attitudes, she resembles male heroes like Achilles. She displays powerful anger, self-assertion and defiance. She believes in retaliatory justice (927-8), faces death with open eyes, and eventually brings it upon herself (cf. 820-21). She is willing to sacrifice her own life to do what is "fine" or "noble" (*kalon*)—a powerful word of approval with aristocratic, heroic, aesthetic and moral connotations (cf. 37-8, 72, 96-7, 925). Like Kreon himself, she is deeply concerned with *timē*—"honor" or status—(5, 21-5, 76-7, 904, 913; cf. 699; for Kreon see 204, 207-10, 284-8, 514-6, 641-4), and afraid of mocking laughter (839-42; cf. 551; for Kreon see 482-3, 647). The converse of this fear is the desire for public recognition, admiration and glory (cf. 72, 96-7, 502-5; also 495-6, 695, 817). When Ismene urges secrecy, Antigone scoffs at her sister and urges her to publicise the deed to everyone (86-7), a desire that shows a need for public acknowledgement not only of the burial, but of Antigone herself. Her desire for glory is also manifested in her final scene, as she goes to her death publicly asserting her rightness and the injustice of her fate (806, 843-9, 937-43).

Antigone shows no interest in marriage and motherhood, which were culturally deemed the primary areas of female concern. It is the "feminine" Ismene, not Antigone, who brings up Antigone's betrothal to Haimon. It is she, not Antigone, who calls Haimon "dearest" and is distressed at the loss of this marriage (568-74). According to Ismene, Antigone herself is "in love" with the impossible (90). In her final scene Antigone does lament that she will never be married, but only in the most general terms (e.g. 814-16, 876-8), without any mention of Haimon or their betrothal. And she goes on to declare her preference for her natal family over any hypothetical husband or child (904-14). Her desire seems to be directed not at Haimon, but towards her dead family members and even death itself (cf. 90, 462-4). Her longing to "lie" with Polyneices is expressed in quasi-incestuous language (73; cf. 897-9). (Similar language is used for a married couple lying together in death at Euripides' *Helen* 985-6.) In the intensity of her grief for him she wails like a bereaved mother bird (422-5), an apt image for a young woman whose passage towards marriage and motherhood seems to have been inverted into an obsessive devotion to the dead members of her paternal family (see further below, p. 95).

As a consequence of her quarrel with Ismene, Antigone is isolated not only from the male, civic world of Kreon, but from her closest remaining female and familial ally, and from the whole world of the living. The rupture in the sisters' initial closeness is expressed dramatically by their divided exits at the end of the prologue. Ismene returns into the female realm of the house, while Antigone departs alone down one of the long entry ramps leading to the external, male world of the battlefield. Throughout the play she is the only female character who will enter or exit by this side-entrance, rather than the house. Her departure provides a vivid dramatic picture both of her transgressiveness and of her solitude. She is repeatedly defined by both herself and others by her separateness, whether chosen or imposed (e.g. 508, 510, 656, 821-2, 850-52, 867-8, 876, 882, 886-7, 941). In dramatic terms, this isolation is further enhanced by the Chorus of old Theban men, who do not arrive until after she has departed. If we are right to view Antigone as the main character of the drama (below, p. 100), this play diverges from the general tendency of Greek tragedy to have a chorus of the same gender as the central character (above, p. 11). The male gender and advanced age of the Chorus give them more in common with Kreon. Although we shall soon discover that Antigone is not alone in her outlook, she herself never learns this. She is not present to hear of Haimon's support or Teiresias' vindication, or to see the fulfillment of the revenge on Kreon that she prays for (927-8).

To a limited extent, the Chorus represents the community at large (cf. above, p. 11). The actors who performed in the chorus were all male Athenian citizens, and the audience, itself dominated by such citizens, would presumably identify to some extent with their peers in the chorus of *Antigone* portraying non-royal members of the civic body. As such the Chorus may be easier for many of the audience to identify with than the extreme, heroic characters who dominate the story. But we should not exaggerate the extent to which they embody "the community." They have been hand picked by Kreon as supporters of the monarchy (164-6), just as Antigone called aside her one potential ally, Ismene (18-19). As male nobility waiting to hear the king's command, they provide a suitable, and suitably public, audience for Kreon's first appearance, in sharp contrast to the secret intimacy of the opening scene.

As we would expect of male citizens without blood-ties to Oedipus's family, the Chorus' point of view is a political one. Their entry-song (*parodos*) is a hymn of thanksgiving to the gods for Theban victory over the attacking army led by Polyneices. The song is pervaded by light—representing life, joy and hope—and distinguished by clarity, sharpness of focus and crispness of sound. There is no moral ambiguity about the battle, no conflict between the laws of the gods and the laws of the city. Evil and impiety are projected exclusively onto the attacking enemy, who are represented as "barbaric," i.e. "un-Greek," in their wealth, bestiality, and arrogance. As such they provide us obliquely with a warning paradigm, reminding us that the gods strike down hard on those who offend them (127-33; cf. 139). The song's aggressive animal imagery (112-14, 117-26) also associates warfare and destruction with an unleashing of animal passions that will turn out to have significance extending beyond this strictly military context.

In the *parodos* the two sons of Oedipus are differentiated only by the all-important political fact that one was defending Thebes and the other attacking. The chorus-members do not judge the brothers' private quarrel, but rather emphasize their unity in duality and the mutuality of their death. This in turn is linked with their incestuous origin, both explicitly and through the use of intertwined language (110-11). We see this incestuous duality repeatedly in the language used to describe the family of Oedipus, with its two sons, two daughters, and various parent-child and male-female pairings, all "natural" dualities that are warped or frustrated by incest, enmity, or death (cf. 4, 12-14, 21-2, 49-58, 61-2, 144-7, 170-2, 512-13, 769).

In Kreon's first speech—which is also his first public utterance as king—he outlines his principles of rule. In contrast to the dialogue of the opening scene, he delivers an extended, uninterrupted speech that projects a sense of authority. There are some disturbing notes from an Athenian democratic perspective, especially in Kreon's emphasis on himself as sole ruler (e.g. 173, 191, 207-210). Some uneasiness may also be felt in his mention of the fact that he won the throne through family ties (174), not just because hereditary kingship was anathema to the democratic Athenians, but because of the past history of the family in question. Antigone has already alerted us to the fact that kinship with the family of Oedipus is likely to be problematic, and Kreon himself has just emphasized the horrible fate of Oedipus' sons, to which he owes the throne. Yet the speech is on the whole dignified and proper. Kreon's first concerns are the gods and the city (162)—a word that will recur numerous times in his mouth. He voices many sentiments that would probably have won general approval from an Athenian audience. His speech is even quoted by Demothenes, a famous fourth century BCE orator, as embodying admirable patriotic sentiments (Demosthenes 19.247-50). The sent=tious utterances that characterize him here and elsewhere can mostly be paralleled from patriotic Athenian sources, and are in themselves impeccable statements of principle. Specifically, there are echoes in this opening speech of the great Athenian leader

Pericles (cf. Thucydides 2.60).

Such general statements of principle, often in the form of clichés or proverbial sayings, are characteristic of Kreon. Yet it remains to be seen how successful he will be at putting these fine generalizations into practice. As he himself says, a ruler's true character can only be seen from how he conducts himself in office (175-7). These three lines echo an old Greek saying, "rule reveals the man." In a sense, they give us a program for the play as a whole: the unfolding events will show Kreon's true character by testing his ability to apply his fine abstract principles to specific concrete cases. After all, it is easy enough to be in favor of "the best counsels" in general terms (179). But identifying what the best counsels are, and carrying them out effectively, may not be so simple (cf. 1265). As we shall discover, the various characters have divergent views on what is "best" and "worst" in life, and consequently on what should guide one's actions (cf. 179, 181, 437, 684, 695, 701-4, 1031, 1050-51, 1113, 1170-71, 1243, 1327, 1331, 1348-9).

The speech displays other linguistic characteristics of Kreon. One of his favorite words is the Greek *orthos*, which means "straight," "upright," or (metaphorically) "correct" (163, 167, 190, 403, 494, 675; cf. 994). (I have translated it as "right," "aright," "rightly," or "upright.") This key word well expresses Kreon's desire to control the world, especially the world of human feelings and behavior, and keep it on a "straight and narrow" path matching his own values and desires. It also accords with his other patterns of imagery, which tend to be drawn from areas of masculine control, such as warfare, animal-taming, metal-work, and sailing, all activities that privilege *nomos* over *phusis* (cf. above, p. 77). There is, however, one striking piece of "natural" imagery in this opening speech, when Kreon first applies his fine principles to "real life," declaring that his edict against the burial of Polyneices is "brother" to his general principles (191-3). The particular choice of metaphor is disturbing, since it recalls the very ties of blood that Kreon is in the process of violating. His own language thus ironically suggests that "friendship" and politics, *polis* and *oikos*, nature and convention, are not so neatly separable as he seems to think.

The Chorus' response to Kreon's speech is characteristically cautious. They do not overtly criticize the edict, but they do withhold their approval, simply remarking that as absolute king, he has the power to do whatever he wants (211-14)—a sentiment that gives a distinctly undemocratic slant to Kreon's exercise of power. They add that no one is "so foolish as to be in love with death" (220), but the prologue has already suggested that they are wrong in Antigone's case (cf. 90). This echo of the prologue accentuates the contrast between the clear and aggressive convictions of the young girl and the cautious, vaguely expressed prudence of these old men. After Kreon furiously rejects their first attempt at advice (278-9), their utterances will be restrained and ambivalent, witholding unequivocal approval from both

Kreon and Antigone. On the one hand, they are Kreon's picked supporters, male members of wealthy aristocratic families, and as such might be expected to side with the king. On the other hand, they are at best lukewarm in their support of Kreon, and are willing to suggest that the gods had a hand in burying Polyneices. Their outlook is summed up in their reaction to Antigone's appearance under guard: "My mind is divided" (376). This ambivalence will persist all the way through Antigone's final scene. Echoing Ismene's attitude in the prologue, they call her behavior "reverent," while at the same time arguing that reverence must give way before power (872-5). They do not assert themselves until Kreon has already crumbled out of fear of Teiresias and asked for their advice (1091-1107).

Even by the standards of Greek tragedy, this chorus is exceptionally unassertive. But their wishy-washiness has clear dramatic value. If the Chorus supported Antigone overtly, this would not only weaken the impression of Kreon's tyrannical grip on power but undermine her isolation. If, on the other hand, they openly supported Kreon, they would be resisting what turns out to be the divine will, and would be in a weak position to urge Kreon to change his mind at the end, not to mention moralizing about his downfall. There are thus good dramatic reasons why their character is so bland and hard to pin down. Moreover their vagueness makes them an apt mouthpiece for the choral odes in this play, which are exceptionally complex, opaque and suggestive.

Kreon's encounter with the Chorus is interrupted by the arrival of the Guard, one of the most distinctly characterized lower class characters in the whole of Athenian tragedy. He is an old man (281), subordinate to Kreon, probably a low-class soldier. He is greatly concerned with his "freedom" (399-400; cf. 437-40, 444-5), which suggests a free man rather than a slave. It is true that Kreon threatens him with torture, which was used only on slaves in fifth-century Athens, but in a mythic milieu this tells us more about Kreon's tyrannical disposition than the guard's social status. If he is a free man, these threats nicely illustrate Kreon's tendency to treat his subjects like slaves (cf. 291-2, 478-9). A further dramatic benefit of viewing the guard this way is that his encounters with Kreon exemplify the bad relationship Kreon has with the common people, as attested by Haimon (688-91).

As a commoner, the Guard not only serves as a reporter of outside events, but provides a vivid sketch of the effects of heroic and aristocratic behavior on subordinates. His values are the inverse of Antigone's (he values his own life and safety above all else; 439-40), and his success or failure are inversely proportionate to hers (her escape would lead to his death; her captivity ensures his freedom). His narrative displays this unheroic character. In contrast to Antigone's unconventional view of the world, he is resolutely commonplace, taking pleasure and pain in the safety or suffering of his friends, but valuing nothing so highly as his own well-being

(436-40). We may compare the Messenger's words valuing personal pleasure above all other goods (1165-71). Though unheroic, these characters
are not exceptionally selfish or hedonistic (such praise of pleasure is common enough elsewhere in Greek texts). Rather they are ordinary people
who, in accordance with the aristocratic ethic of noblesse oblige, are not
held by themselves or others to the same moral standards as the heroic
figures. They provide an ordinary human outlook against which the actions and passions of the great and mighty may be measured, for better or
worse.

The Guard provides a measure of Kreon as a ruler not only of noblemen (the Chorus) but of ordinary people as well. The soldiers' collective
fear of Kreon (268-77), along with the king's furious reaction to the news of
the burial, reveals a tyrannical personality that was only latent in his opening speech. When the Chorus suggests that the gods may have had a hand
in the burial (278-9), he reacts as if his entire status as king were under
threat, equating any disagreement with political rebellion. Using language
that would certainly be disturbing to a free Athenian democrat, he speaks
of his political opponents as animals whose necks should be kept firmly
under the "yoke" of his rule (289-92). His suspiciousness, and his threat of
torture to the guard (306-9), further confirm this tyrannical outlook. He
reacts with equal fury to the high-status Chorus and to the low-class Guard,
perceiving both as challenging his own nobility and power. As the play
progresses, we shall see him being equally defensive when various other
aspects of his identity are perceived as threatened.

Another distinctive feature of Kreon's character is illustrated by his
immediate assumption that whoever buried the body was motivated by
money or profit (293-303). Throughout the play he uses financial imagery
in a way that suggests a narrowly contractual and materialistic view of the
world (e.g. 221-2, 310-14, 322, 324-6, 1035-8, 1045-7, 1055-6, 1061-3). This
may be contrasted with the use of such language by others to attribute
value to non-material goods. Haimon and Teiresias will both claim that the
greatest "possession" for mortals is good sense (683-4, 1050), Teiresias that
learning from others is "most sweet" and can bring "profit" (1031-2), and
Haimon that the greatest "possession" and "treasure" for a father and son
is their mutual good fortune and reputation (701-4). Even the Messenger
rejects the value of material wealth in comparison with happiness (1168-
71). Antigone, like many tragic heroes, goes even further, actually invert-
ing the conventional application of terms of material value. Thus she declares that for someone in her situation death itself is "profitable" (462-4;
contrast the Chorus at 220 and the Guard at 439-40). Similarly she juxtaposes a radically different kind of "good sense" to Kreon's narrowly calculative view of rationality (cf. e.g. 469-70, 904, 1050-52). Haimon offers yet
another kind of "good sense," one that is rooted in nature (683, 712-17), but
allows for learning and is open to all human beings (705-11, 719-23). By

this standard Kreon himself lacks good sense, as Teiresias will confirm (1015-16, 1023-7, 1043-52). As a result Kreon ends with "stored up" property consisting in nothing but misery (1279), a situation where no "profit" can be found (1326-7).

The first Guard scene is followed by one of the most famous choral songs in the whole of tragedy, the first *stasimon*. In this song the Chorus obliquely continue to express their amazement at the extraordinary act of burial of which they have just heard. Their attitude towards it is typically ambivalent. On the one hand, it is one of the "awesome" human acts that they seem to be extolling (332-4). Yet they warn that human daring can lead to harm as well as good (365-75), and their reaction to Antigone's arrest is one of horror at her transgression of the law (376-83). But the themes of the song extend far beyond this specific dramatic moment, reaching to the heart of one of the play's most fundamental themes: the proper place of human beings in the world as a whole.

The first three quarters of the song extol the amazing achievements of reason, which has given human beings mastery over the powerful natural phenomena that threaten our existence, by means of such skills as sailing, agriculture, hunting, language, architecture and community life (332-64). The human race is represented in this song as using rational skills to control nature (the sea, the earth, animals and harsh weather) to its own benefit. Since ancient Athens was a patriarchal culture, the human subject presupposed here is the male, and most of the activities enumerated are masculine ones. Reason is the faculty by which human beings—especially men—are most often distinguished from animals.

Yet this praise has undertones of ambivalence. For example, in Greek texts sailing often connotes the reckless pursuit of excess wealth prompted by greed. And agriculture is described in the song itself as "wearing away" the Earth, "the highest of gods" (338-9). Earth, the mother of all gods and mortals, represents the power of the female, especially the procreative power that gave women their most significant role in Athenian life. Women are often likened to the earth (cf. 569) or to wild animals (cf. 424-5, 433). Imagery of plowing, taming and yoking is frequently used for the subordination of women to men, specifically by means of sex and marriage (cf. 569, 827-8, 946-7, with notes). The verb "lead," used in the song for the taming of animals (346), suggests a man taking a woman in marriage (below, p. 94-5), and may also be used for taking prisoners, like Antigone herself (e.g. 381, 395). Yoking imagery is used for other relationships of subordination as well, such as ruler to subject (cf. 292), or god to mortal (cf. 955). There are therefore implicit questions here about the right way for men to treat women as well as the rest of the "natural" world, and the right way for all human beings to behave as subordinates of the gods.

The ingenuity that enables us to control our world can also lead to the downfall of humans and their communities (365-72). What, then, are the limits of human, and specifically masculine, control? The song offers no explicit answers, but there are suggestive links to other strands of imagery in the play. The character who most obviously tries to exert rational control over natural phenomena like kinship and death is Kreon. Like "man" in the song, he looks forward to life and the future, he is practical, self-motivated, and attempts to create and control his own world. Antigone, by contrast, looks backwards in time, to her dead family members and the long-standing laws of the gods; she seeks to maintain this traditional world with her bare hands and her convictions rather than ingenuity and tools. As we have seen, Kreon's speeches are full of controlling imagery, which is directly linked both with anxiety about gender and with a tendency to treat his subjects and his family like slaves (473-5). Haimon, by contrast, will argue for a more harmonious and yielding relationship to family members, fellow citizens, and the natural world (701-23). Such passages develop the themes of the first *stasimon* and suggest that although its overt reference is to Antigone's deed, its implications apply equally to Kreon. Most obviously, it is Kreon who starts out "high in his city" but then falls (370).

The song conjures a world in which the extremes voiced by both Antigone and Kreon are integrated, the exercise of human control over the nature is constrained, and the "laws of the earth" in both senses (human laws and the laws of the underworld) are respected along with the laws of the gods, resulting in harmony and prosperity for both *polis* and *oikos* (368-75). The *polis* is important, indeed vital to human prosperity, but it is made up of and situated in a web of relationships to other people, the gods, and the forces of the sustaining earth. The particular resources of lyric poetry are highly effective at conveying this sense of a world where competing forces are integrated rather than polarized. For example, the phrase translated as "the impulse to civic law" (355) consists of two words in Greek, one of which (the noun *orgas*) refers to human tempers, dispositions, or passions, especially anger, which are usually innate, while its accompanying adjective (*astunomous*) combines a word for the city with the word *nomos*, which suggests both law and rational human organization (above, p. 77). In Greek the two words are closely linked through grammatical agreement. This untranslatable phrase uses linguistic interconnections of a kind unavailable to English in such a way as to convey the inseparability of these different aspects of human life. Such a world-view is alien to the polarized extremes occupied by both Antigone and Kreon.

The song ends as the Guard returns with Antigone, who has been arrested for burying the body a second time. As with the first burial, there are hints that the gods have been involved, by sending a quasi-miraculous dust-storm to conceal Antigone's movements (cf. 421). This is typical of the way in which gods usually accomplish their will in Greek mythology, not by direct action but by inspiring and assisting human agents. The dust-storm suggests that the earth itself, like the "earth gods" that Antigone reveres, is angry and is working as her accomplice. It also suggests a natural world out of balance as a result of Kreon's edict. The storm is a "trouble" and a "sickness," causing earth to occupy an alien element—the air—and blighting healthy natural growth (417-21).

Many commentators have worried over the fact that Antigone repeats the burial, when the proper ritual effect has been achieved by doing it the first time. But the repetition is both dramatically useful and psychologically convincing. On the dramatic level, it enables Sophocles to show us Kreon's reaction to the burial while we, the audience, know who has done it but he does not. (This technique is known as dramatic irony, and is highly characteristic of Sophocles.) It also allows him to give us the heightened drama of Antigone being caught red-handed, and to delay the confrontation of the two protagonists. On the psychological level, it is perfectly plausible that Antigone, with her passionate, strong-willed nature should revisit the corpse with a pitcher for libations and rebury it when she sees that it has been uncovered.

At last the two central characters are brought into direct confrontation. But they will never make moral or intellectual contact—a separation signalled dramatically by Antigone's refusal to meet Kreon's eyes (441). In fact, this scene will provide the only direct interaction between them in the entire play. Kreon usually speaks of Antigone in the third person, even when she is present (e.g. 480-5, 561-2, 567, 883-90), and as she goes to her death Antigone does likewise (914-19, 927-8, 942) In this scene, however, they both briefly address each other as "you." Antigone does so in response to Kreon's accusation that she has broken the law, belittling his specific decree in comparison with the immortal and unwritten "laws of the gods" (450-60). The phrase "unwritten laws" appears elsewhere in Greek, referring not to codified law but to ancient customs and traditions that cannot be attributed to any human inventor. Antigone does not specify the exact content of the "unwritten law" to which she is appealing, but an ancient audience would probably assume that she is referring to the powerful traditional obligation of families to bury their dead.

Antigone invokes the laws of the gods in general, but the gods with whom she is most preoccupied are those of the underworld (cf. 73-7, 89, 451, 521), especially Hades, king of the dead (cf. 519, 542). These gods, who live under the earth, are known as chthonian or "Earth" gods, and are associated with birth and fertility as well as death. As such they are appropriate divinities for Antigone, preoccupied as she is with the family, since the *oikos* includes all its members, past as well as present and future, and is deeply concerned with the proper treatment of the dead. Apart from Hades, most of the powerful Earth gods are female, including Gaia or Earth herself (cf. 339), Persephone (cf. 894), and the Furies, goddesses of vengeance (cf. 603, 1074-5). Kreon, by contrast, is focussed on the *polis*, which is primarily concerned with practical decisions concerning the immediate welfare of its living members. He is a pious man in his own way (cf. 162-3, 198-201, 288-9). He is aware of the dangers that pollution for family blood-shed may pose for the *polis* (773-6), and ends up obeying the advice of the prophet (1095-7; cf. 991-7). But his primary concern, as a ruler, is with the living, not the dead. Accordingly his attention is focussed on the "Heavenly" gods, who live in the sky upon Mount Olympus. They are ruled by Zeus (184, 304; cf. 758), a patriarchal king who is the divine counterpart of Kreon himself. Not surprisingly, Kreon sees Zeus as a ruler in his own image, assuming that he and the rest of the gods will support his own view of the world, including his political outlook (282-9).

Yet the divine realm cannot be so neatly packaged. Greek polytheism acknowledges the complexity of the human world and its many competing claims upon us by providing many different, often overlapping, functions for the gods. One cannot safely concern oneself with just one aspect of the divine world, or with one god to the exclusion of others. Olympian Zeus is not only the ruler of the sky gods, but protector of the hearth and family, and in this capacity Kreon will defy him in blasphemous terms (486-90, 658-9, 1039-43). Kreon is also contemptuous of Antigone's reverence for Hades, ruler of the dead (777-80). But here again he is too narrow in his focus, since Zeus himself could be equated with Hades (see note on line 452). This failure to understand the multivalence of the gods, and of Zeus in particular, ironically leads Kreon to muddy a clear distinction that the gods themselves hold dear—the distinction between the proper areas of concern of the gods of earth and sky (1067-76).

Kreon makes no response to the particulars of Antigone's defense. Sophocles could easily have given him him a strong defense of the principles of human law, but chooses not to. Instead he makes Kreon react with a fury that is expressed in part through further generalizations about human nature and authority (473-9). His controlling imagery recalls the the first *stasimon*, but in a more harsh and confrontational manner. And he shows again his inability to apply his worthy maxims to a specific case in a reasoned fashion. His images for the over-rigid spirit that is easily shattered will turn out to fit himself more closely than Antigone (cf. below, p. 99-100). The same applies to his attitude towards those who harbor "mighty thoughts" (478-9; cf. 1351-3).

By implying that Antigone is his slave (479), Kreon further confirms his tyrannical attitude to ruling both as a king and as a patriarch. As with the Chorus and the Guard, he views Antigone's defiance as an attempt to usurp his royal power. But there is an important additional element. This time his fury is prompted by what he perceives as a threat to his authority not only as a king and a nobleman, but also as a man (484-5). Since there is a homology between political rule and patriarchal rule, gender is explicitly factored into his conception of kingly power (525, 677-80). He treats gender as a zero-sum game, in which a woman who asserts herself against a man makes that man himself into a woman (484-5), and a man who defends a woman becomes less than a woman (740, 746, 748, 756), therefore a fortiori less than a "real" man. Even sex and marriage are viewed in strictly calculative and militaristic terms, as risky pleasures that may end up "wounding" a man (648-52; cf. 571). In light of these attitudes, it is hardly surprising that Kreon tries to keep women in their "proper place," inside the house (578-9).

Such hostility towards women finds many parallels in ancient Greek texts, but Kreon's is unusually pervasive. The particular character of his misogyny is bound up with his defensiveness about other aspects of status besides his masculinity, namely kingship, fatherhood, and age (cf. below, p. 93). It is difficult to gauge the probable response of Sophocles' original, predominantly male, audience, to a character of this kind, or to the woman who confronts him. Different audience members would no doubt react in different ways. On the one hand, the outcome of the play is obviously in an important sense on the side of Antigone. There are signs that she wins the approval not only of the gods, but of the city (692-8). Moreover she is acting in a situation that has been provoked by male mismanagement, and in which there are no male family members to take appropriate action on her behalf. Yet one cannot but wonder how many Athenian men would be comfortable with this female assertiveness. Such anxieties may have been allayed, however, by the fact that Antigone ends up dead as a result of her "unfeminine" behavior, and is elided from the conclusion of the play. There is no word of her after the report of her death, which is itself subordinated to that of Haimon in the Messenger's narrative (1208-43). She serves here as a catalyst for a tragic confrontation between men. By the end of the play, the transgressive female has been permanently hidden from sight within the earth, her "female" home. The reestablishment of political order seems to require the silencing and concealment of women like Antigone. Responsibility for the disruption of such order is left on the shoulders of the male ruler, where it belongs.

The confrontation between Kreon and Antigone descends into the cut-and-thrust of stichomythia (single-line dialogue) (508-25). This dramatic pattern, with opposed speeches breaking down into stichomythia, is a frequent one in Greek tragedy and especially in this play, which is structured round a series of such confrontations. As a formal device, stichomythia is especially effective for crystalizing divergent points of view. In this case the exchange sharply articulates two sets of opposed values: Kreon is concerned about the living (508-10), Antigone about the dead (515, 521); Kreon assumes the permanence of enmity (514-16, 522), Antigone of friendship (523); Kreon cares about the brothers' treatment of their homeland (518), Antigone about their blood-ties to herself and each other (511, 517); Kreon is concerned with the political (518), Antigone with the "natural" (511, 523). These ideological differences are sharpened by the verbal echoes between their lines (e.g. "view" in 508-9, "shared" in 512-13, "friend/enemy" in 522-4; cf. also "reverence/irreverent" in 511, 514 and 516 and "below" in 521 and 525). This kind of verbal echoing is a frequent feature of stichomythia, with rhetorical victory going to the speaker who caps the other's lines (cf. esp. 726-57.) For the most part, it is Antigone who caps Kreon in this passage, marking her as the winner of their verbal dual. It is true that Kreon has the final word, when he tells her to go and practise "friendship" down in Hades (524-5). But although his control of crude physical power enables him to "win" in this obvious sense, the way he exercises that power will rebound upon his own head, leaving Antigone the moral victor.

In the course of this exchange Antigone famously declares that her nature "joins in friendship, not in enmity" (523). There is some doubt, however, about her rejection of enmity, even among kin. The prologue showed no such rejection in principle (cf. 10, 86-7, 93-4), and in the next scene she will harshly reject Ismene when she tries to share the blame (or credit) for the burial. Antigone's rejection of her sister has the purpose of saving her life (553), but this is not something Antigone herself views as a benefit (462-4), nor does Ismene claim to desire it (548). And Antigone's manner towards her sister is distinctly hostile. From here on, she will speak and act as if Ismene did not exist (cf. 895, 941). This enables Antigone to maintain her heroic emphasis on singular, conspicuously glorious action (cf. 546-7). It also suggests that her devotion to "friendship" is limited to dead members of her paternal line—it is among the dead, she claims, that enmity has (perhaps) been abolished (521). This obsession with the dead (cf. 559-60) also coheres with her silence during the stichomythia between Ismene and Kreon, in which we learn from Ismene of Antigone's betrothal to Haimon (568-75).

The precise tone of this scene is hard to pin down. It can be played many different ways. But we should not evade the harshness it suggests in Antigone's character. It is important for dramatic reasons that Antigone should not be a perfectly lovable heroine, just as it is important that Kreon have some good qualities. Kreon becomes progressively more tyrannical throughout the play, yet he displays appropriate values for a king at the outset, and seems to retain a sincere concern for the *polis* (cf. 776). He also arouses our sympathy at the end of the play for his pain and remorse as a broken man. Antigone, by contrast, though clearly right from a religious point of view in her basic commitment to burying her brother, is portrayed as harsh, unforgiving, and as unconcerned as Kreon is with the perspectives of people and values besides her own. In drama, as in life, a person may be right about one thing and wrong about others, and being right or wrong is not correlated in a straightforward way with a character's emotional appeal. Otherwise the play would become a melodrama, featuring a clear-cut villain and hero, and would lose much of its complexity and power.

This applies to the minor characters as well: Ismene, Haimon, and even the Guard are all designed to arouse a complex response of sympathy, pity, approval and / or disapproval in an audience.

Kreon despatches the two girls into the house, and the Chorus sing another densely-packed ode. This song, the second *stasimon*, meditates on the terrible doom of the house of Oedipus. Like the first *stasimon* it is rich with images of the natural world, this time a world that is seriously out of control from a human perspective. The primary image for the fate of the house of Labdakos is a terrible storm, which gives further resonance to storm and sailing imagery used elsewhere in play: the ability of "ingenious man" to control the stormy sea in the first *stasimon* (335-8); Kreon's reliance on the "ship of state" (162-3, 188-90); and Haimon's warning that the rigidly controlling steersman will capsize his ship (715-7). This song reminds us that the family as well as the *polis* may be viewed as a storm-tossed ship, a fact to which Kreon remains blind until he is crushed into recognizing the power of the "harbor of Hades" (1284). It associates this upheaval in the natural world with the anger of the gods, the stamping out of fertile growth in the family line, irrational frenzy, the dust and darkness of burial and the underworld (593-603). This complex of images suggests, in contrast to the opening of the first *stasimon*, that human ingenuity is not, after all, equal to controlling natural forces.

The conclusion of the song also echoes that of the first *stasimon*. In the earlier ode the Chorus sang of how human ingenuity can bring us either to evil or to good (365-75). In this one they sing of how human beings may confuse good and evil under the influence of divine hostility and dangerous passions (615-25). The stated cause of these pernicious passions is "hope" (615). In English, hope is a positive concept, but in ancient Greek the nearest equivalent word (*elpis*) has a wider range of meanings. It may mean "hope" in a positive sense (897, 1246), but may also be used for a neutral expectation or even a negative foreboding (cf. 330, 366). *Elpis* may benefit us by its encouragement, but it may also be foolish and even dangerous, since our irrational desires may provide false optimism about the future and thus lure us to disappointment and ruin (cf. 221-2).

As with the first *stasimon*, the surface application of this ode is to Antigone, the direct descendant of the Labdakids who is now overcome by "doom." But hope and the pernicious passions it causes are said to belong specifically to men (616). And the image of the man who proceeds in ignorance until he burns his foot (618-19), though it will find an echo in the Chorus' evaluation of Antigone (853-5), is far more obviously applicable to Kreon. Furthermore, he is the one who is ultimately shown to have wrong-headed ideas about the difference between good and evil (622-4). The ode has resonances for Haimon as well. He, after all, is the one who will be "cheated" by hope and erotic passion (616-7; cf. 629-30).

The storm and fire imagery in this song, together with the attribution of disaster to "senseless words and a Fury in the mind" (603), suggests an equation between the forces of the natural world and the irrational passions of human beings. This is sustained elsewhere in the imagery of the play. Kapaneus' hostility and Antigone's own passionate feelings are both likened to blasts of wind (137, 929); Kreon's threats are like a winter storm (391); Ismene's and Niobe's tears of anguish are like stormy rain (526-30, 829-32; cf. also 541). In the second *stasimon* the epithet "light-headed" (617), used for the desires arising from hope, provides a specific echo of the first *stasimon*, where it was used for the light-hearted but empty-headed birds (342). These associations add retrospective significance to earlier animal imagery. For example, Kreon's taming imagery (473-79) may be read in terms of the relationship between human reason and the passions. His decision to give up Polyneices' body to dogs and birds of prey may be seen as echoing Polyneices' own brutality (cf. 110-26, 198-206), as a deed prompted by passion, and as a departure from the norms of "rational" or civilized human behavior. Along with the complex of images in the second *stasimon*, all this suggests that the "ingenious man" of the first *stasimon* may have as much trouble controlling human passions as the violent world of nature. These passions are the form in which the "storms" sent by the gods have their most devastating impact.

At the end of this ominous song Haimon enters and tries to persuade Kreon to change his mind. He starts out as a model of tact and courtesy (635-8, 685-7, 701-4). But Kreon immediately requires him to take sides. He declares that a son's sole role is to support his father in all things—a demand for unconditional allegiance that sits uneasily with his devaluing of "natural" blood ties. The bond of marriage is likewise to be considered only in strictly utilitarian terms (639-54). Kreon's lack of respect for Haimon's feelings about his marriage echoes his earlier response to Ismene. When she first mentioned the betrothal, Kreon replied, "there are other plots of land for him to plow" (569). Such agricultural language is not unusual in reference to Athenian marriage (see note on 569). But Kreon's tone shows an exceptional lack of sensitivity to the personal aspects of the marital relationship, as Ismene's response indicates (570). It is also, in Ismene's view, insulting to his son, since it "dishonors" him by neglecting his opinions and wishes (572). Kreon thus takes a crudely calculative and disrespectful view of two central familial relationships: the parent-child bond and the bond of marriage. He goes on to apply a military standard to both these relationships, making Haimon into a dutiful soldier with an obligation of absolute obedience, and Antigone, as "woman," into the "enemy" of them both (648-80; cf. 740). It remains to be seen, however, whether the military model favored by Kreon, the "general" (8), is also the best model for "ruling" a household, a wife, or a city at peace.

Haimon shows himself to be his father's son in his ability to wield maxims (683-4, 701-4, 707-11, 719-23). He also uses Kreon's favorite word *orthos* (636, 686, 706), and the metaphor of the ship of state (715-7). He thus knows how to speak his father's language. But the world-view he offers is a very different one, as signalled in his opening suggestion that "things might also turn out well some other way" (687). He speaks eloquently of flexibility (710-23), and encourages respect for others: for one's children (701-4), for the views of one's subjects (692-9), and for anyone who may be wiser than oneself (705-9, 723). He pictures a world where the passions are not at odds with rationality, or *polis* with *oikos*, where the interests of himself, his father, his fianceé, and the gods can be harmoniously integrated (cf. 748-9). This is economically expressed by his retort that he is siding with a woman, "if you are a woman" (741). But this, of course is an egregious insult in Kreon's eyes, as it would be for any Athenian man (cf. e.g. Aeschylus, *Agamemnon* 1625). He reacts as we have seen him do so often, as someone threatened in his authority, as a king (733-8, 744), as a man (740-41, 746, 748, 756), and this time also as an older man (726-7) and as a father (742). As before, this passionate fury will be instrumental in sealing Kreon's doom, since it provokes Haimon into running off, never to return (760-65).

Haimon said nothing at all about his personal feelings for Antigone, but the Chorus immediately launch into a choral song (the third *stasimon*) which attributes the dispute between son and father to erotic passion. Haimon's subsequent behavior will show that there is truth in this interpretation of events. He proves unable to take his own advice about yielding to circumstances and bending with the wind, illustrating instead the Chorus' words about Eros and madness (790; cf. 632). But this does not mean we should view his entirely reasonable arguments towards Kreon as hypocritical. Certainly they are an effective rhetorical strategy under the circumstances, but that does not make them dishonest. Like most major characters in Athenian tragedy, Haimon displays a complex layering of various and sometimes conflicting motives, both rational and emotional, for his behavior. We have no reason to doubt his claim that he is concerned about everyone involved—Kreon and the *polis* as well as himself and Antigone (748-9).

Like other characters in this play, Haimon starts out as a model of rationality, but subsequently emerges as driven by powerful emotions. Ismene refused to participate in the burial on grounds of rational prudence, but reappeared in a state of passionate grief and tried to share in the death she earlier rejected. Kreon too begins many encounters in a reasonable vein, but ends by breaking into passionate anger. Teiresias, like Haimon, begins with rational discourse and ends in passionate rage, abandoning his considered resolve to keep silent about Kreon's approaching doom (1060). Eurydike, Kreon's wife, whose sole role in the drama is to kill herself and thus compound her husband's misery, starts out as a highly reasonable women (1190-91, 1246-50), but departs to kill herself out of passionate grief

and rage (1301-5). Even the Chorus is diverted from their cautious prudence, caused to break their own moral boundaries, by the terrible sight of
Antigone going to her death (803-5).

Eros, along with his mother Aphrodite and the wine-god Dionysos,
is one of the great forces of irrational passion. As such he is a powerful and
dangerous god, whose influence is to be dreaded rather than sought out
(cf. 790). He places human beings on a level with wild animals through the
irrational power of passion (782-90). Even the immortals are subject to him
(787), making him even stronger than the power of death that subdues
"ingenious man" (361-2) but cannot subdue the gods. Such forces are barely
controlled by reason, the morally ambiguous rationality that was the subject of the first *stasimon*. That song celebrated the human ability to tame
nature. But the drama as a whole suggests we may be less successful at
taming the passionate nature that lurks within ourselves and others. Echoing the first two *stasima*, with their reflections about what makes us turn to
evil rather than good (above, p. 85-6, 91), the ode on Eros tells us it is passions such as erotic desire that turn the minds of the just to injustice and
thus destroys them (791-2). Kreon's view, expressed near the beginning of
the play, was that money has this effect, twisting the minds of good people
to criminal behavior (297-301). But the evidence of the drama suggests otherwise. Not a single character is motivated by money. Rather, all are driven
by passionate emotions, no matter how successfully they rationalize their
behavior. Above all, Kreon's own passsionate temper leads him into dire
error and prevents him learning from others until it is too late.

The Chorus' ode to Eros evokes a wedding celebration, especially in
its emphasis on the erotic attraction between bride and groom (795-7).
Marriage is the culturally sanctioned institution for expressing and controlling the dangerous forces of Eros and Aphrodite, and a wedding would
be an appropriate occasion for extolling their power. Choral song and dance
form part of wedding celebrations as early as Homer (*Iliad* 491-6). In a way,
then, this *stasimon* is a substitute for the marriage song and dance that would
have been performed at the wedding of Haimon and Antigone. As such it
introduces a symbolic "marriage" procession. At its conclusion Antigone
is led out of the palace, like a bride leaving her father's house to be led to
that of her new husband. The Chorus makes the analogy explicit, com-
menting on Antigone's passage to "the bridal chamber where all must sleep"
(805).

Antigone's own song of lamentation develops this theme, making
her passage to death into a kind of inverted marriage ritual, in which she
sings her own "wedding song" to accompany this "marriage" procession.
While lamenting her loss of a real marriage (e.g. 867-8, 876-82), she views
herself as being led away to become the "bride" of Hades, king of the underworld (811-16; cf. 575, 654, 891, 1205). The way she speaks of him "putting her to sleep" also suggests "taking to bed," as a bridegroom takes a

bride in marriage (811; cf. 805, 833). The verb "lead," used repeatedly in this scene (e.g. 812, 885, 916, 931, 939), is the standard word for a husband "leading" a woman from her father's house to his own in the ritual marriage procession. Sometimes the subject of these verbs is Kreon himself (773, 916). He will not literally be the one who "leads" her to prison, but the servants who perform this task are treated as extensions of him rather than separate agents (773, 916). This places him in the symbolic role of bridegroom, in a manner that befits the perverted erotic relationships of this family. It also equates him with death itself, which suits his role as one who belittles the human relationships of marriage and parenthood that ensure the perpetuation of the family.

The idea that a girl who dies before marriage is marrying death is a common one in Athenian tragedy and in Greek culture generally. The mythic archetype for this is Persephone, who was stolen away from her mother by Hades and married to him in the underworld. In real life there were many striking similarities between funeral and marriage rituals, especially from a woman's point of view (e.g. both involve torches, processions, a veil). The epitaph of a girl who dies unmarried often speaks of her tomb as her marriage chamber. All of this makes sense if we think of both occasions as major rites of passage, in which a woman is taken from the house of one man (her father or other male guardian) to that of another (her husband or Hades). Both are radical changes of state or status, since marriage may be viewed as the death of a girl's virginity, or of her former unmarried self. But the poignancy of the parallel resides precisely in the fact that marriage, though an occasion for anxiety in the young bride, is also a time of great societal rejoicing. When marriage is replaced by death, the ritual that should lead to the incorporation of an outsider (the bride) into the *oikos*, and its renewal through reproduction, has become instead the means to destroy it by preventing its regeneration.

In her final scene Antigone reiterates her intense dedication to her dead family members (891-9). This makes the theme of "marriage to death" peculiarly appropriate in her case. Her inverted "wedding" involves a return to the family of her birth, the family from which a young woman is normally separated by marriage. Her dedication to her (dead) natal family is thus a denial of the culturally prescribed passage of a girl away from that family towards the family of her husband and the new life of motherhood. She is returning to the earth that bore her, and will never be a "woman" in the full cultural sense of becoming a wife and mother. As far as we can infer from the text of the play, she will never leave the underground cave in which she is united to her natal family and "married to death" in a sterile, childless union. This accords with her tendency to characterize herself in negative terms which emphasize deprivation and loss, and the generally negative tone of her rhetoric (e.g. 4-6, 69-70, 450-60, 511, 515, 517, 538-9, 543, 546-7, 850-52, 876-82, 905-7, 916-20). She is a figure less of positive ideals than of resistance and denial.

Antigone's rejection of marriage in favor of her natal family also helps to contextualize the notoriously strange explanation she now provides for her action in burying her brother. She claims that she would not have performed this deed for a husband or child, since these are replaceable, but only for a brother, who is not (904-14). This passage has troubled many critics because it seems to violate Antigone's earlier expressed commitment to the burial of all dead kin. But in fact, Antigone never articulated any such commitment to *all* kin, even though that is what the original audience no doubt assumed. She simply declared that she was following the "unwritten laws" of the gods (450-60). She did not specify precisely what this might entail, but went on to focus on burying her brother as her own flesh and blood (466-7). Her later argument favoring brothers over a husband or child coheres well with her unwavering commitment to the dead in preference to the living, and her lack of interest in Haimon or Ismene. It also suits her general preference for the "natural" (blood-kinship) over the "conventional" (the human institution of marriage). Her assumption that the gods condone her choice suggests that, like Kreon, she views them in her own image.

Critics have also been troubled by the rationalistic, calculative tone of the argument. But as we have seen, all the characters are driven by a complex of rational and passionate motives, producing rational arguments to justify behavior that turns out to be driven also by irrational passions. Antigone is no exception to such rationalizations. As early as the prologue she uses a kind of emotional or ethical calculus when she says she cares more about pleasing the dead than the living because she will be obliged to spend more time with the former than the latter (74-6; cf. 89). A similar tone informs her self-defense, where she calculates the relative "profit" and distress of dying versus leaving her brother unburied (460-8). This does not necessarily undermine the honesty or validity of that defense. Rather, it shows how a person may act from a powerful combination of motives, whether emotional, ethical, or rational, which may be intertwined and expressed in a variety of ways. Nor is such calculation necessarily unheroic. Antigone's words at 460-61 recall Sarpedon's classic enunciation of the heroic code of honor in the *Iliad*, where he declares that it is only because human beings must die some time that it is worth risking one's life for glory (12.322-8).

Besides being an inverted wedding, Antigone's final scene is simultaneously her funeral. Like her "marriage," this "funeral" is a perverted one, since she is being buried alive. In her last song she mourns her own passing, and also provides her own funeral eulogy. At this point she finally provides some acknowledgement of the importance of the city. Like Ismene in the prologue, she seems to equate Kreon's edict with the will of the citizens as a whole (905; cf. 79). And by calling the land and city of Thebes, and its most prominent citizens, to witness her fate (843-9, 937-43), she implies that her actions and sufferings do after all have public implications. Her lamentation uses language that suggests the inextricability of city and family (806-7), and interweaves many of the polarized themes of the play: family, gods, city, land, war, wealth, *nomos* (840-49). This goes some way towards mitigating the one-sided narrowness of her perspective and acknowledging the interdependence of family and *polis*.

Antigone's final words as she departs are in anapests, the meter most often used to end Greek tragedies (937-43). This gives a sense of closure to her portion of the drama, even though the fact that the anapests are spoken by herself, not the chorus, makes it clear that this is not the end of the play. Her protracted funereal exit as she is led away down the side-entrance leading to the plain—the same path she took earlier—is accompanied by a choral ode still more dense and opaque than those that preceded. In a kind of funeral-wedding song, the Chorus introduce various mythic parallels for her situation—a common technique in choral songs. In this they are developing Antigone's own earlier comparison of herself to Niobe, who offended the gods and was turned into stone, but still continues to weep (see n. on 826). Unlike Antigone, Niobe was above all a mother devoted to her children. Yet Niobe's strange death makes her an apt mythic exemplar for Antigone's unique state, belonging fully neither to death nor to life, a grotesque amalgmation of a living human being with the natural world.

The Chorus provide three more mythic parallels for Antigone's case. Their song is exceptionally hard to interpret because the details of the stories, presumably familiar to the Athenian audience, have been lost to us. Moreover the cases cited do not seem to parallel Antigone's very closely, except for Danae, an innocent girl who was imprisoned by her father to prevent her from marrying (944-50). All the examples, however, involve some kind of enclosure or prison, like the cave in which Antigone will be entombed. Parent-child violence and perverted marriage are also significant themes of at least the third example (979-80). But as in the earlier songs, there are implications for Kreon as well as Antigone. Even the Danae strophe concludes with the moral that fate cannot be deflected by money, warfare, or ships (951-4)—three realms of masculine activity with which Kreon rather than Antigone is preoccupied. There is also the alarming paradigm of Lykourgos, a man "quick to rage," who was punished with madness for resisting the god Dionysos (955-65). Kreon is manifestly "quick to rage," and Haimon has accused his father of being raving mad (764-5). In a particularly suggestive detail, we hear that Lykourgos tried to prevent women's ritual behavior (963). And the curious language describing the "yoking" of Lykourgos (955-9) suggests the kind of emasculation that will shortly be visited upon Kreon (below, p. 103).

This song is followed by the entrance of the prophet Teiresias. Like Haimon he expresses good will towards Kreon (992-5, 1031-2), and emphasises flexibility and learning (1023-32). His lurid description of the failure of his rites of prophecy powerfully conveys the sense of chaos, the disruption of divine and human distinctions and categories, that has resulted from Kreon's decree. Verbal echoes reinforce the close tie between the failed sacrifice and the rotting state of Polyneices' body (cf. esp. 410, 906, 1008). The dead have been left unburied above the earth, and the living are entombed within it. The institution of blood-sacrifice is a ritual means of reaffirming human beings in their proper relationships towards gods, animals, the natural world and each other. Failed sacrifice is thus a powerful expression of the disruption of such relationships. Sacrificial victims should burn, not ooze with moisture (cf. 1005-11); the altar is not the proper place for human flesh (cf. 1016-18); animals should serve as victims, not as "tombs" for human bodies (1021-2, 1080-83). The rituals surrounding death and sacrifice have been confused and perverted like those of death and marriage (above, p. 94-5).

Besides the interpretation of sacrifice, the main channel of communication between gods and mortals is the practice of augury (interpretation of bird-signs). Birds are messengers between gods and mortals, as Kreon is well aware (1040-1). The breakdown of relationships between gods, mortals, and the earth is therefore further expressed in the incomprehensibility of the bird-song that is the prophet's guide to the divine will (999-1004). Instead of sending clear signs to Teiresias, the birds are twittering "incoherently," or more literally, like foreigners who do not know Greek ("barbarians") (1002). The language of non-Greek speakers is elsewhere likened to the twittering of birds (e.g. Aeschylus, *Agamemnon* 1050). Foreign language and bird-song alike are viewed as inarticulate, mindless chattering, in contrast to the clarity and intelligence on which the Greeks prided themselves. Hence the need for the specialized prophet, who is able, through divine dispensation, to decode the twittering of the birds into meaningful signs from the gods. The physical blindness of Teiresias is correlated with a more powerful inner vision that enables him to "see" and "read" these signs where others cannot. Kreon, by contrast, is morally blind. His approach to the tomb, and gradual deciphering of his sons' cries and their meaning, is a kind of grim parody of prophetic sign-reading (1206-18; cf. 631). Because of his behavior, effective communication between parents and children as well as gods and mortals has been stifled (cf. 757).

Teiresias' repeated use of the word "sign" (998, 1004, 1013, 1021) recalls the guard's original description of the burier of Polyneices as "one who left no sign" (252). Unlike "man" in the first *stasimon*, who violates the earth with his plowing (338-41), Antigone has left the earth unmarked. Paradoxically, this absence of the expected human signs of the work of burial is itself a sign—a hint of divine involvement in the burial. So too the failure of Teiresias' bird-signs, and the "signless" sound of Haimon's inarticulate voice (1209), are clear signs of the gods' displeasure. Kreon's violation of the proper order of the living and dead has disrupted the human ability to attach signs to their meanings in an articulate or reliable fashion. A similar breakdown of rational human communication is exemplified by the way both Haimon and Eurydike become silent in their passionate grief (1231-2, 1244-5). As the Chorus and Messenger remark, such silences may themselves be frought with meaning (1251-2, 1256).

The Teiresias scene is closely parallel in structure to the earlier scene with Haimon. In both cases an unexpected new arrival enters, tries to persuade Kreon to change his mind, provokes the king's anger, retaliates with threats, and departs in a fury (compare esp. 766-7 with 1091-2). The main difference is that after encountering Teiresias, Kreon does finally give in, seeking and then following the advice of the Chorus. Why does Kreon finally yield? There was a hint after the Haimon scene that he might be open to persuasion from the chorus (770-71). But his primary resolve is not shaken until he hears the words of the prophet. Kreon is a man with great respect for hierarchy. And unlike all those who have previously clashed with him (Antigone, Ismene, the Chorus, Haimon and the Guard), Teiresias has a claim to superior authority. He is not younger, subordinate, a woman, or Kreon's son, but an aged and revered representative of the gods who has helped Kreon in the past. Even though Kreon's first reaction is one of defensive and even blasphemous wrath (1040-41), he attempts to restrain himself in an unprecedented fashion, at least momentarily (1053; compare Haimon's respect for his father at 755).

Teiresias predicts Kreon's punishment using the kind of economic language that Kreon best understands: he will give up his son as "a corpse to pay for corpses" (1067; cf. also 1077-9). He will suffer from the gods the same kind of retaliatory justice that he inflicted on Polyneices and Antigone (1074-6), and it will take a similar form: the violent and untimely death of those who are closest to him (1064-7). His attempts to suppress female "wails" of mourning (28, 204; cf. 423, 883-4) will be repaid with "wailing cries" in his own house (1079; cf. 1207, 1227, 1303, 1316). Teiresias also broadens the picture beyond the family to embrace the well-being of the *polis* (1080-83), something Kreon has never stopped caring about, however wrong-headedly.

These predictions induce Kreon to capitulate, out of fear, not considered judgement (1095-7; cf. 997, 1113). The ruler who views the world through a military lens has realized that the ultimate victor is the gods, or "necessity," which he can neither defeat nor control (1106; cf. 361-2, 799-800), though he still does his best to do so one last time, declaring confidently that he will rescue Antigone (1111-13). He is scared into respect for "the established laws" (1114), thus finally learning Antigone's lesson (cf. 453-5), and fulfilling his own prophecy that the most rigid spirits are most easily shattered (473-9). Antigone, at whom this gibe was directed, will end up dead, but her spirit is never broken. She never changes her mind or yields in her convictions. Kreon remains alive, but he gives in to fear and ends up crushed with grief and repenting of his previous choices.

Both Kreon and Antigone are one-sided, willful, destructive of themselves and others, and blind to other points of view. These are common features of the heroic character, especially in Sophocles. But the fact that Kreon ultimately yields has led many critics to view Antigone, who does not, as the "real hero" of the drama. Yet although yielding makes Kreon in some ways less heroic, it also makes him more human. He becomes a different kind of tragic figure, one who makes amends too late rather than resisting to the end. His remorse and the destruction of his former self lead to an increase in emotional stature, arousing the pity and sympathy of the audience. Moreover from the perspective of the play as whole, Kreon not only has the largest part, but drives and unifies the drama, which is framed by his edict and his downfall. He is a more fully developed character than Antigone, shown as king, tyrant, father, and eventually crushed victim of his own folly. The latter portion of the play is entirely focussed on him and his misery. He also displays certain qualities often found in tragic heroes: he is the one whom successive characters attempt to dissuade (cf. e.g. Oedipus in *Oedipus at Colonus*) and who faces a moment of painful decision between two evils (1096-7; cf. e.g. Agamemnon in Aeschylus' *Agamemnon*).

It is therefore perhaps less helpful to try to identify the "real" hero of the play than to view it as a tragedy of two focal characters and their interrelationship, characters who are constituted and defined by their differences, but whose very differences give them meaning in relation to each other. One of these characters, Antigone, closely resembles other "Sophoclean heroes." The other, Kreon, shares some of the same qualities, but is best seen as a different kind of "hero," who suffers a different kind of tragic downfall. In any case, the particular tragic outcome of this play is the result of neither one of them alone. What is most significant is their duality, their mutual need for each other as complementary agents in the generation of tragedy, an interdependence that replicates on the level of dramatic structure the tragic, incestuous dualities of the house of Oedipus (above, p. 81).

The Chorus sing one more song, exhorting Bacchus (Dionysos), protector of Thebes, to come and save the city of his birth. On a different level, the Athenian citizens who make up the Chorus are themselves singing and dancing in honor of Dionysos, god of the theater. So when they address Dionysos as a chorus-leader (1146) we may detect a moment of close identification between the chorus of Athenian citizens and the Theban elders that they portray. As Theban worshipers they invoke Dionysos optimistically, praying for him to come and heal or "purify" the city's "sickness" (1141-5; cf. 1015-16). But ancient methods of healing were often very painful, involving surgery and cautery—cutting and burning—without any anaesthetics. And like all Greek gods, Dionysos is ambiguous in his gifts and powers. A god who brings healing may also bring destruction, sometimes simultaneously. We have already seen the dangerous power of irrational forces in this play, and Dionysos is among the greatestof such forces. He is a god of fire and night (1146-54), of madness and transgression, whose myths involve kin-murder and the rending and eating of raw flesh (sometimes human). His more sinister aspects have been just hinted at earlier in the play. In the *parodos* the Chorus used his revelry as a metaphor for Kapaneus' assault (135-6), and celebrated him as the "shaker of Thebes" (154). Later they sang of his punishment of Lykourgos with madness (955-65). In this final song they refer to the torches used in his worship (1126), which are often a symbol of destruction (cf. 135-7, 1146-7), and to his mother Semele, who was killed by lightning (1139-40). The city will indeed be "healed," but only at the cost of disaster for its ruling family.

As the Chorus end their prayer, the Messenger enters to tell us of Antigone and Haimon's suicides. The two young people are finally "married," physically united in Antigone's "bridal-cave of Hades" (1205). Antigone has hanged herself with a fine piece of fabric, probably her veil (1221-2), a symbolic item in marriage rituals, which in this context also suggests a shroud. Hanging is a frequent method of suicide for women in Greek myth (cf. 53-4), especially for virgins, since it leaves the body unpenetrated. (Married women responding to the violent death of a son or husband are more likely to use a sword, as Eurydike will do: 1301-2.) Men commit suicide much more rarely than women, but when they do so, they typically use a sword, as Haimon does. His death is described in a highly eroticized fashion. As he plunges the sword into his body he simultaneously embraces the passive Antigone with his dying breath, spurting blood upon her cheek in an image that combines defloration with ejaculation (1234-41). (For the cheek as a locus of erotic desire see 784; cf. also 530.)

Haimon's extreme passion makes him a counterpart, in a perverse way, of Antigone. In keeping with a zero-sum conception of gender, the apt mate for the assertive, masculinized woman is the passive, feminized man. Haimon's subjection to Eros, his extreme emotion, his inarticulate wailing cries, his silence and his choice of suicide are all "feminizing" traits. There is a particular analogy between him and Ismene. Both are passionately devoted to Antigone (compare especially 491 and 632, where the same rare word is used); both attempt in good faith to persuade one of the conflicting principals to yield to better judgment and submit to forces greater than themselves; and both are harshly repudiated by the person they attempt to persuade. In Kreon's view, his son's support for Antigone makes him even lower than a woman (740, 746, 748, 756). His attempt to mediate between the values of *polis* and *oikos*, *erōs* and patriarchy, male and female areas of concern, ends with his own destruction.

The Messenger's narrative is also heard by Eurydike, Kreon's wife. She is introduced into the story, perhaps for the first time by Sophocles, only to complete Kreon's punishment by dying with a suicidal blow that echoes Haimon's (1301-2, 1315-16). (Her name, which means "wide justice," may have been chosen to fit this role.) Like Antigone she is a woman whose life, and whose aspirations as a wife and mother, are destroyed by Kreon. Like Antigone, she sides with blood-ties over marriage, wails in mourning and curses Kreon (compare especially 424-5 with 1301-5). In contrast to Antigone, however, she is clearly marked as a "good woman," a wife and mother devoted above all to her children (1282, 1301-5). She remains invisible within the house until Kreon's disruption of the "natural" order brings her into view (1180-91; cf. 1248-9, 1293). Her silent return into the house (1244-5), and her subsequent suicide, are "proper" ways for a dignified woman to respond to disaster.

Eurydike's death takes place at the altar, in the very heart of the house. (This may have been revealed to the audience through the device of the *ekkuklēma*; see p. 73, note 2.) It thus symbolizes both the revenge and the downfall of the *oikos*. She achieves this revenge not only through her own death but through her dying curse and the presence of her polluting body on the household altar (cf. 1080-3). She thus completes Kreon's devastation through the very forces of family for which he earlier showed such disrespect. His relationship to the dead Haimon and his dead wife recalls the quasi-incestuous, quasi-erotic death embrace that unites Antigone with her dead family members and Haimon with Antigone (1173-7, 1263-4, 1289-91). Like Oedipus before him, he has destroyed himself through his unwitting violations of the bonds of parenthood and marriage (cf. 1340-41). By cutting down the "last root" of the house of Oedipus (600), he has also destroyed the last seed of his own house. He has become a child-killer (1173, 1304-5, 1312-13, 1340), and a wife-killer (1341), a destroyer of his own marriage and future lineage as well as Antigone's and his son's. These are the same personal ties that Antigone belittled in her final speech, when she said that she would not have risked her life to bury a husband or child. But Antigone spoke from a position of ignorance, never having experienced such ties herself. As a husband and father, Kreon was in a position to know differently. He will learn what it really means to have a wife and child, but only at the cost of their destruction.

By the end of the play Kreon has been symbolically stripped of every facet of his identity, as a king, a father, and a mature man, to which he clung so defensively. It is appropriate that someone with such a rigid and authoritarian view of status should be punished by the loss of his own status and authority. As early as his confrontation with Haimon there were hints that he did not deserve the social status that accrue to manhood and mature age (cf. 735, 741). After the Teiresias scene he became a man who obeys commands instead of giving them (1099, 1107-8; contrast 734). In the Messenger's narrative his status relative to his son was reversed when he debased himself through supplication (1230). In the final scene, this debasement is complete. As someone who "exists no more than nothing" (1325) he lacks any kind of human status at all. This last phrase suggests that his punishment also symbolically matches the offence of inappropriately confusing the living and the dead (1066-73; cf. 849-52, 871, 885-90). Now that Antigone is dead and Polyneices buried, there is no confusion between life and death for them. Like Antigone, Ismene, Haimon and Eurydike, Kreon now longs to die in his turn (1308-9), but must live on as the "living corpse" of which the Messenger speaks (1167; cf. 1325). He himself says the news of his wife's death has "re-killed" a "dead" man (1288), just as he himself, in Teiresias' words, "re-killed" Polyneices (1029-30). Like Antigone, he receives his epitaph while still alive (1161-7).

As befits Kreon's preoccupation with manhood, his final debasement is expressed in terms of gender inversion. He enters in a funeral procession that reverses Antigone's departure, performing the predominantly female role of highly emotional lyric lamentation over a dead child. There is a subtle ambiguity in the way he speaks of his wife's death as a "woman's doom" embracing him (1289-91). His wording not only recalls the erotic death-embrace of Haimon and Antigone, but suggests that Kreon himself has been feminized by his fate. As a man, he has become "worthless" (1339). Finally he is "led away" like a bride or a prisoner (1323-4, 1339), in a further dramatic mirroring of Antigone's own last exit (compare especially 1323-4 with 885-6). But whereas Antigone was led away from the palace and out of the city, Kreon finally goes into the house, the female realm (see p. 75, n. 2), which will entomb him in solitude like Antigone's cave.

The Chorus' final words concerning divine repayment for "mighty words" (1351-3) evoke the boastful attackers of the *parodos* (127-33; cf. also 478-9). The king who tried to do his best for the *polis*, the "general" (8) who succeeded in defending it from external enemies (1162), has turned out to be the enemy within. Although Kreon attributes this disastrous outcome to a god, or to "destiny" (1273-5, 1296, 1346), he nevertheless takes full responsibility for all his actions (1268-9, 1318-21; cf. 1112-3). The Chorus likewise speak of inescapable "fate" (1337-8; cf. 235-6), but still assign full responsibility to Kreon himself (1259-60). They are at least as hard on him as they were on Antigone (1270; cf. 853-5). This accords with the predominant world-view of Greek culture and mythology. The gods are involved in our lives, but we must still accept full responsibility for our own choices— for better or worse. Kreon's failure is an offense against the gods, but it is also a failure in human terms, a failure of human communication and co-operation, which causes his downfall. Unlike the solitary Antigone, Kreon started out surrounded by advisors and well-wishers. But his attempts at inappropriate control, his inability to listen and respect the advice of others, stripped him of friends and rendered him as ineffectual as an isolated non-person (cf. 739, 757, 764-5).

Ultimately Kreon fails to control anything, even the death of Antigone, who remains a law unto herself until the bitter end (cf. 822, 875). The word *orthos* returns at the end of the play to provide a corrective to the narrow and rigid view of the world that generated this failure. The Chorus comment on the "rightness" of Teiresias (1178; cf. 99), and the Messenger informs us that it is no human being, but "fortune" that sets human life "upright" and dashes it down again (1158; cf. also 1195). Kreon's insistence on "rightness" has been disrupted by the gods, who can effortlessly "toss" human affairs any way they wish, taking sides with the forces of nature, including human passions, in order to do so (cf. 162, 583, 1274; contrast 291). The result is that everything Kreon holds in his hands at the end of play is "warped" instead of straight (1344). But as Kreon crumbles, the ineffectual Chorus becomes increasingly assertive (1098-1107, 1270, 1334-5), suggesting at least the possibility of a form of rule more open than his to persuasion and advice from the citizen body. As usual in Greek tragedy, it is this collective body, the Chorus, who voice a final moral, a cliché whose triteness is redeemed by the profound complexities of the drama we have witnessed.

BIBLIOGRAPHY

This is only a tiny sample of the innumerable works devoted to Greek tragedy, Sophocles and *Antigone*. It includes works cited by author and date in the text, together with others chosen for their interest and accessibility to the English-speaking reader.

Cultural and Religious Background

Burkert, W. *Greek Religion* (Eng. trans. Cambridge, Mass. 1985)

Buxton, Richard. *Imaginary Greece: The Contexts of Mythology* (Cambridge 1994) [the cultural contexts of myth-telling]

Dodds, E.R. "On misunderstanding the *Oedipus Rex*," *Greece and Rome* 13 (1966) 37-49; reprinted in E.R. Dodds, *The Ancient Concept of Progress* (Oxford 1973) and E. Segal (ed.) *Greek Tragedy* (New York 1983) [useful on guilt and pollution]

Ehrenberg, V. *From Solon to Socrates* (2nd ed. London 1973) [history of the sixth and fifth centuries with a cultural emphasis]

Fantham, E., H. Foley, N. Kampen, S. Pomeroy and A. Shapiro (edd.). *Women in the Classical World* (Oxford 1994)

Howatson, M.C. (ed.). *The Concise Oxford Companion to Classical Literature* (Oxford 1993)

Tyrrell, William Blake and Frieda S. Brown. *Athenian Myths and Institutions* (Oxford 1991) [the uses of myth in Athenian culture]

Books on Ancient Greek Tragedy

Buxton, R.G.A. *Persuasion in Greek Tragedy* (Cambridge 1982) [a useful account of an important aspect of drama]

Csapo, Eric and Slater, William J. *The Context of Ancient Drama* (Ann Arbor 1995) [surveys all the evidence for the ancient theater and production]

Goldhill, S. *Reading Greek Tragedy* (Cambridge 1986) [an introduction from the perspective of contemporary critical theory]

Jones, John. *On Aristotle and Greek Tragedy* (London 1962) [challenges the view that character is central to Greek tragedy]

Kitto, H.D.F. *Greek Tragedy* (3rd ed. London 1961) [a provocative and still valuable introduction]

Lesky, A. *Greek Tragic Poetry* (Eng. trans. New Haven 1983) [a thorough survey of tragedy and scholarship]

Rehm, Rush. *Greek Tragic Theater* (London 1992) [a good introduction from the perspective of performance]

——————————. *Marriage to Death* (Princeton 1994) [a detailed exploration of this theme in tragedy]

Taplin, O. *Greek Tragedy in Action* (London 1978) [a fine introduction to tragedy in performance]

Vickers, B. *Towards Greek Tragedy* (London 1973) [makes good use of mythic, social and religious background]

Wiles, David. *Tragedy in Athens: Performace Space and Theatrical Meaning* (Cambridge 1997) [the use of theatrical space to create meaning]

Wohl, Victoria. *Intimate Commerce: Exchange, Gender, and Subjectivity in Greek Tragedy* (Austin 1998) [a contemporary feminist approach]

Books on Sophocles (all include some discussion of *Antigone*)

Blundell, M.W. *Helping Friends and Harming Enemies: A Study in Sophocles and Greek Ethics* (Cambridge 1989) [discusses Sophocles in the context of Greek popular morality]

Bowra, C.M. *Sophoclean Tragedy* (Oxford 1944) [old-fashioned but still valuable for its learning]

Bushnell, Rebecca W. *Prophesying Tragedy: Sign and Voice in Sophocles' Theban Plays* (Ithaca, NY 1988) [interpretation using the theme of prophecy]

Gardiner: C.P. *The Sophoclean Chorus: A Study of Character and Function* (Iowa City 1987) [looks at the chorus as a character]

Gellie, G.H. *Sophocles: A Reading* (Melbourne 1972) [an accessible introduction]

Kirkwood, G.M. *A Study of Sophoclean Drama* (Ithaca 1958) [good on character and aspects of dramatic technique]

Knox, B.M.W. *The Heroic Temper* (Berkeley 1964) [influential and readable account of the Sophoclean "hero"]

Reinhardt, K. *Sophocles* (English trans. Oxford 1979) [demanding but influential]

Scodel, R. *Sophocles* (Boston 1984) [a stimulating introduction]

Seale, D. *Vision and Stagecraft in Sophocles* (London 1982) [visual aspects and imagery of sight]

Segal, C.P. *Tragedy and Civilization: An Interpretation of Sophocles* (Cambridge, Mass. 1981) [a detailed structuralist account]

Waldock, A.J.A. *Sophocles the Dramatist* (Cambridge 1951) [refreshingly iconoclastic, if often wrong-headed]

Webster, T.B.L. *An Introduction to Sophocles* (Oxford 1936) [old-fashioned but still useful, especially on Sophocles' life]

Whitman, C.H. Sophocles, *A Study in Heroic Humanism* (Cambridge, Mass. 1951) [dated but often stimulating]

Winnington-Ingram, R.P. *Sophocles: An Interpretation* (Cambridge 1980) [an outstanding study by a sensitive scholar]

Studies of Antigone

Else, G.F. *The Madness of Antigone* (Heidelberg 1976) [detailed study of irrational aspects of character]

Foley, Helene P. "Tragedy and Democratic Ideology," in *History, Tragedy, Theory*, ed. B. Goff (Austin 1995) p. 131-50 [a balanced approach to the Athenian political context]

——————————. "Antigone as Moral Agent," in *Tragedy and the Tragic*, ed. M.S. Silk (Oxford 1996) p. 49-73 [relates moral decision making to gender]

Goheen, R.F. *The Imagery of Sophocles' Antigone* (Princeton 1951) [a valuable and detailed study of systems of imagery]

Murnaghan, Sheila. "*Antigone* 904-920 and the Institution of Marriage," *American Journal of Philology* 107 (1986) 192-207 [places Antigone's final speech in an anthropological context]

Neuburg, Matt. "How Like a Woman: Antigone's 'Inconsistency'," *Classical Quarterly* 40 (1990) 54-76 [a compelling defense of Antigone's last speech]

Oudemans, Th.C.W. and A.P.M.H. Lardinois. *Tragic Ambiguity: Anthropology, Philosophy and Sophocles' Antigone* (Leiden 1987) [a very detailed structuralist study]

Segal, C.P. "Sophocles' Praise of Man and the Conflicts of the *Antigone*," *Arion* 3 (1964) 46-66 [a subtle account of the play's conceptual ambiguities]

Sourvinou-Inwood, C. "Assumptions and the Creation of Meaning: Reading Sophocles' *Antigone*," *Journal of Hellenic Studies* 109 (1989) 134-48 [a controversial attack on Antigone and defense of Kreon]

Steiner, G. *Antigones* (Oxford 1984) [looks at later treatments of the story]

Zeitlin, Froma. "Thebes: Theater of Self and Society in Athenian Drama," in *Nothing to Do with Dionysos?* edd. J. Winkler and F. Zeitlin (Princeton 1990) 130-67 [examines the use of Thebes as an "anti-Athens"]